HOW TO TALK TO YOUR DOG

Bill Habets

How To Talk To Yur Dog
Bill Habets

Copyright © MMXI The Windsor Group

Published MMXI by The Windsor Group
Hamilton House,
2 Station Road,
Epping
CM16 4HA

Typeset by SJ Design and Publishing, Bromley, Kent

ISBN   978-1-903904-73-2

Contents

Foreword

In a show-stopping number from the musical Doctor Dolittle, the main character proclaims at length his fervent desire to 'talk with the animals', making it clear 'oh, what great fun that would be!'

Original though the lyrics are, the sentiments they express are, of course, nothing new as mankind has since time immemorial longed and strived for the ability to communicate with members of other species. And of all the different kinds of animals that exist, it is almost certainly the dog with whom most people have wanted to, as it were, 'converse'. It is hardly surprising that this should be the case, because, after all, it is the dog who has been recognised throughout history as being man's best and most faithful friend, despite the rival and no doubt equally vocal claims others may put forward on behalf of the horse or the cat.

No, in most people's minds – and this is certainly a view shared by readers of this book – whatever may be the doubtless merits of our equine or feline companions, it remains a truism that a dog is man's best friend.

There is, as always, another side to that particular coin, and that is that man should also equally be dog's best friend. This, sadly, is not always the case. All too often our pets, although greatly loved by most of us, can at times be somewhat neglected – not so much in the physical sense, but because we have somehow failed to understand them fully. However, this lack of effective communication is not something that should surprise us. After all, people often have major difficulties in truly understanding each other, even when they speak the same language.

This book has been written to help you understand your dog better by recognising and correctly interpreting his 'talk', that is the myriad of signals he is sending you all the time – and at the same time also help your dog understand *you* better, something that will be achieved when you learn the best way to express yourself so that what you're trying to convey is in a form that makes sense to his mind. As, gradually, you and your dog establish better ways of communicating, you really will become your dog's best friend under all circumstances, because it is only through being aware of how your dog reacts, thinks and sees his world that you can truly look after his needs – including his emotional ones as well as the more obvious physical ones – properly.

There is nothing quite like the bond of affection that links a caring and understanding owner with his dog. And to forge this bond it is important to be able to empathise with your dog ... that is to see things from his point of view. As your mutual understanding grows, you will almost certainly also develop an intuitive reasoning, a sort of sixth sense, as to how your dog reacts and this, in turn, will allow you to care better for him. Your reward for this, of course, will be a happier dog and it goes almost without saying that a happy dog in turn means a happy owner.

Given half a chance, your dog will be your most loyal and adoring companion, always ready to share in your joys and sorrows. Invariably, no matter how much you may give him, you'll always receive more in return. If you consider how much friendship he gives you, his demands upon you are relatively small – food, shelter and, ideally, as much affection and understanding as possible.

In closing this foreword, I would like to ask the reader's indulgence as I dedicate this book to Clyde, my very own best four-legged friend, whose special insight has made such a major contribution to my efforts.

Bill Habets

Chapter 1
Can A Dog Really Talk?

To answer the question that heads this chapter, one needs first to look at what exactly is meant in this context by the verb 'talk'. And when seeking to define a word, the obvious place to start is naturally a dictionary, and here is what the Collins English Dictionary has to say about it:

Talk: to express one's thoughts, feelings, or desires by means of words (to); speak (to)

However, more relevant to us at this moment, is the second definition that Collins also provides:

Talk: to communicate or exchange thoughts by other means, and then cites as an example of this usage the phrase *lovers talk with their eyes*.

Obviously, there is no doubt that dogs do talk – and most clearly as well – according to the second definition, as we shall discover in depth in later chapters in the first part of this book. Just the same, that still leaves less than fully answered the directly-related question as to whether dogs can express themselves through the use of words.

In many ways, the jury is still out on that question. Until not so long ago, the generally held view was that dogs could not talk in the sense that they used words to convey meanings, but recent scientific studies have caused the experts to think again.

A UNIVERSAL INTER-SPECIES LANGUAGE?

In fact, the latest discoveries are strongly suggesting that not only can dogs talk but that a wide variety of species – including humans while they are still babies – share what might be called a universal, although extremely primitive, language that is common to all of them in many aspects. And, say the researchers, there are strong and unmistakable correlations between means of vocal expression as dissimilar as the barking of dogs, the tweeting of birds, and the cries of human babies.

The most recent research into this inter-species language comes from Peter Pongracz, a professor of ethology – that's the study of the behaviour of animals in their normal environment – at Eotvos Lorand University in Budapest, Hungary. In the first part of their project, Professor Pongracz and his team investigated how accurately people of different backgrounds were to able to ascribe meanings to previously recorded series of dog barks. The barking sounds – from a Mudi Hungarian herding dog – were those made by him while in several distinct emotional states, including happiness, playfulness, aggressiveness, fear and despair.

The response of the listeners to the barks were then compared to acoustic models of the barks that revealed in detail the tone, pitch, and duration of each sound as well as how much time elapsed between each successive sound in a given series.

When all the results were analysed, it became clear that the listeners had in more than three quarters of their answers accurately identified how each bark related to an emotional state. Interestingly, the listeners scored best of all with interpreting low-pitched barks separated by very short intervals as being aggressive and high-pitched barks with considerably longer intervals as being essentially non-aggressive.

Fascinating though these findings were, they took on an extra dimension when the various acoustic qualities of dog barks were then compared to the cries of human babies expressing similar emotions. "The sound quality characteristics of dogs and human babies are broadly similar, almost uncannily so," said Professor Pongracz, "although there is one marked difference: with babies, the frequency range appears more important than pitch alone."

So it seems that very young humans begin life endowed with a primitive communication language of sorts that to a large extent is similar to that used by both young and adult dogs, making it a fairly good bet that babies may also have a substantially greater ability to recognise the meaning of dog barks than adults. The upshot of this is that various scientists are now testing the theory that we may have had an instinctive ability to better understand animals when we were very young and this ability gradually dissipated, perhaps largely because of disuse, as we learned human language. The idea of an innate talent that eventually is 'lost' as part of the growing up process is of course not all that strange. For example, it is well known that most babies can swim to some extent, but lose – or 'forget' – this ability, unless they are regularly given opportunities to swim, as they grow older.

COMMON SOUNDS SHARED BY MANY MAMMALS

Just as startling in its implications is the further recent discovery that it is not only young humans and dogs that appear to have a common approach to verbal communication but that this system of expression through sounds may well be shared to greater or lesser extents by just about all mammals. For example, another study concluded that in the vast majority of cases young children, aged up to about eight years, had little difficulty in identifying the underlying emotions in macaque calls.

The common verbal link between emotions and the resultant emitted sounds has been noted in many different species in the past. Although the actual sounds may vary greatly – such as the bark of a dog, the song of a bird, or even the mooing of a cow – the common denominator always seems to be that pitch or frequency, as well as how long sounds are separated from each other, indicate certain emotional states.

There are two quite separate explanations why the sounds of different species – although similar in many respects – vary so greatly in their actual content.

To begin with, there is the theory that was first put forward by noted international avian expert Eugene Morton. Essentially, he argued, in accordance with the general laws of physics, larger bodies would produce sounds that were primarily characterised by an abundance of low frequencies, while sounds of higher frequencies would be produced by relatively small bodies. With some exceptions, such as the neighing of a horse, the validity of this view is obvious to the most casual of observers. Incidentally, Mr Morton further suggested that this link between the body size of an animal and their sounds could often be extremely useful to the 'listening' animal because it could use this information to help predict the likely size of the 'sender', so aiding it to determine whether it was likely to be a predator big enough to pose a potential risk.

The second explanation as to why animal – and human – sounds vary so greatly is that the arrangements of the organs that produce sound vary greatly among species. A typical example of this is the immense physical difference between humans and dogs that makes it impossible for dogs to produce many of the sounds that together constitute any human language.

While most people think of talking as something that is mainly done by their mouth, we actually use many other parts of our bodies as well, including the vocal cords, a variable air supply from the lungs, and even a head that is shaped the right way to allow the produced sounds to be emitted correctly. Certainly most people do not know that the configuration of their cranium greatly influences the sounds they can produce, because it serves as a kind of sounding plate for a large number of the non-percussive primary sounds that are such an essential part of our language.

Were a dog to strive to imitate the sounds of any human language, that attempt would be doomed to failure from the start. Because, try as he might, a dog simply doesn't have the physical equipment to do the job, lacking, amongst other things, a head of a suitable shape, and his vocal cords and the air pipe that leads to them just cannot produce anything resembling the sound of human words.

However, this physical restriction imposed by Nature upon the ability of dogs to speak in words that we can understand without effort does not mean that, providing you're prepared to put in a little bit of effort, you will not be able to interpret correctly the sounds that your dog produces. And to help you in this task, researchers have noted a curious development: dogs living with humans for any length of time appear subtly to change – perhaps 'adapt' is the more correct description of the process – the sounds they produce, this thought to be a likely result of them trying to imitate within the limits of their physical abilities words from human languages.

Apart from the changes occurring in the communications skills of specific dogs because of the way they live with humans, there is yet another important factor at work, and that is, as research has shown, that the many centuries of domestication have altered how dogs seek to communicate. Studies have found that there are massive differences between how today's domesticated dogs express themselves compared to how their ancestors, the wolves, convey the same emotions. Incidentally, these changes don't just affect vocal-type sounds but also the visual signals sent out by dogs, including how their faces display a variety of 'looks'.

THE ANSWER TO TWO QUESTIONS

Summing up these findings, Professor Alan Beck, director of the Center for Human Animal Bond at Purdue University, said there was little doubt that pet dogs were able to communicate with their human owners through their barks. "And, of course, as dogs and humans share some basic non-verbal communication, it is likely that verbal ones also exist."

Coming back to the original question – can dogs *really* talk? – the overall evidence is overwhelming that the answer has to be a resounding 'yes', providing you accept that *verbal communication* – which, after all, is just a phrase that describes 'talking' in another way – is equivalent to talking even when the sounds it relies on are not necessarily what we humans think of as words.

Once you accept that your dog can indeed 'talk' to you in many different but perfectly understandable ways, the next question that will almost automatically pose itself is: to what extent can dogs *understand* the words we use? After all, Dr Dolittle's stated ambition was to 'talk *with* the animals', not merely talk *to* or listen to them.

In many ways, this is a much easier question to answer, because as every dog owner knows, his pet will almost invariably respond – although not always in necessarily the most appropriate way – to words spoken to him, this proving that human language holds some meaning for him. How you can train your dog to understand what you say more easily – and, just as importantly, how you can adapt what you say so he will have a considerably better chance of interpreting it correctly – will be explained in depth later in this book. In the meantime there are two key facts that set the scene for different ways of achieving true and meaningful two-way communication, verbal and otherwise, between you and your dog. These are:

1.   The average domestic dog has a wide range of sounds, as well as other ways of sending signals, that you can learn to interpret correctly without too much effort; and

2.   Equally, the average domestic dog has the ability to learn to 'make sense' – within limits, of course – of much of what you say.

The net result of these two basic conclusions is that it's perfectly possible to greatly improve such two-way dialogue as may already exist between you and your pet. As will be explained in later chapters, all that's needed for this to happen is a little bit of knowledge, some effort, and a fair amount of patience on your part.

While you'll find the required knowledge in this book, you'll have to supply the effort and patience yourself. However, your reward for doing so will be immense: you and your dog will both be able to 'talk' to each other!

Chapter 2
How Dogs Talk
To Each Other

As we have seen in the previous chapter, there are many different ways through which dogs can express themselves. Some of these are pretty obvious and it doesn't take a great deal of deductive effort to understand them; the meaning of many others are, however, considerably less than immediately clear.

It is obvious that when you are trying to assimilate what to you is a foreign language – whether this is Albanian, Hopi, or, as in this instance 'dog talk' – it can be immensely useful to have some knowledge of the context in which that language is used, as this will offer many clues as to the sort of things its 'native' users will usually want to express. For example, it is said that the Eskimos have more than twenty different words for 'snow", each of them denoting the very specific qualities of a certain type of snow. Naturally, the nature and qualities of a particular kind of snow can be incredibly important to Eskimos living in the traditional way and it is therefore essential to them to distinguish between its various forms, something that matters relatively little to the rest of us, whose vocabulary therefore doesn't encompass these fine nuances and who generally have little interest in describing whether or not today's snowfall is suitable material for building igloos or not.

What the above example illustrates is that human language evolves to enable its users to communicate with each other about those things that are pertinent to their daily lives, and a broadly similar pattern can be observed when studying how other species communicate. Bird song can warn of predators nearby; buffaloes will stamp the ground with their hooves to send a message of imminent danger to the rest of the herd; and it probably wouldn't be all that fanciful to suggest that cows may well have 'moo' variations to indicate diverse types of grazing.

Accordingly, applying the above principle to dog talk, you would expect canine language to be rich in those forms of expression that are likely to be of the greatest everyday use to them. At least that's what logic would suggest, and in this instance logic is right, except that the answer its application suggests only tells a small part of the story, because an immense – perhaps the largest – part of your dog's vocabulary is not linked to its current way of life as a domestic pet but is instead inherited from its ancestors. It follows from this that to begin to understand how today's Fido or Rover acquired their communication skills, you have to look well beyond their current way of life and consider how their forebears lived in the distant past.

HOW TODAY'S DOGS EVOLVED

As is generally known, modern dogs are descended from wolves, and as might be expected much of any dog's instinctual behaviour – including how it communicates – is still based on that of its forefathers many times removed. So deeply ingrained by inheritance are many of the traits of modern dogs that it pays us to look at how these came about in the first place. Therefore we have to turn back the clock and begin our quest for a deeper understanding by examining how it happened that dogs first joined forces with man.

There is considerable dispute amongst scientists about when

man and dog first established a symbiotic relationship. Until fairly recently, the mainstream view, based primarily on archaeological discoveries, was that the first ever domestication took place somewhere between 10,000 and 14,000 years ago. But the latest research, only made possible by recent advances in DNA technology have now cast severe doubt on these dates, and there is currently strong evidence to suggest that dogs first became domesticated more than 100,000 years ago, meaning that the man-dog relationship could be nearly as old as modern man.

The drastically revised date is the result of studies carried out by a team of international geneticists, led by biologist Robert K. Wayne, of UCLA, who analysed the DNA mutations of 140 purebred dogs and 162 wolves, as well as that of five coyotes and eight jackals, the latter included for comparison purposes. What astounded the researchers is that they found substantially more mutations than they had originally expected, all these extra mutations, they said, pointing inexorably to the fact that a much longer span of time would have been needed for them to occur than hitherto thought. Taking into account the extra time it would have taken for the additional mutations to evolve, the scientists concluded that it was at least 100,000 years ago – maybe even considerably longer – since man and dog first started sharing their lives.

ONLY A SINGLE COMMON ANCESTOR

Incidentally, the same research also proved conclusively once and for all that dogs only have one common ancestor – the wolf – as they do not share DNA with either jackals or coyotes. Previously, many biologists had thought that some breeds of dogs could have been the product of other genetic lines as well.

Although it is likely that the argument about exactly how long ago man domesticated the first dog is likely to continue, two things are absolutely certain: whether that happened 10,000 or

100,000 years ago, the dog is the oldest of all the domesticated species, and the basis of that domestication was the realisation by both men and dogs that such a relationship could work to their mutual benefit. Essentially, the original bargain struck between the two species was straightforward enough: man would supply the dog with food, shelter, protection against predators, and companionship; in return, the dog helped man in a wide variety of endeavours, including tracking game and other hunting-associated tasks, as well as providing guard and warning duties.

As the centuries rolled by, the domestic dog began to evolve – chiefly because man selectively bred them to reinforce particularly useful traits, this marking the starting point of the many breeds that exist today – and a good deal of the behavioural characteristics it had inherited from its wolf ancestry began to become less obvious, these replaced to a large extent by man-induced conditioning. However, while many of the underlying wolf-like patterns eventually faded further and further into the deeper recesses of the dog's consciousness, two major inherited traits still have a major influence on the everyday behaviour of today's modern dog:

1.   The dog is a 'territorial' animal'
2.   It is also a 'pack' animal.

WHAT IS A 'TERRITORIAL' ANIMAL?

Let's begin by considering exactly what is meant by saying that dogs are 'territorial animals'? Essentially, it means that dogs have very specific areas they regard as *their* territory and will defend these against whoever they perceive as trespassers, interlopers or threats. Stated so simply this behaviour may not seem all too significant but it provides the explanation for much of your dog's behaviour.

In fact, wolves, our pets' ancestors, had two quite different types of territory: a large one over which they hunted and this might well measure a hundred square miles or even more; and a considerably smaller 'home' area that was more fiercely defended than the bigger one.

Similarly, your dog also recognises two kinds of territory. First, there is the bigger general area of your neighbourhood that he knows from his walks and then there is his 'home' territory, generally represented by your home and garden. The way your dog reacts to otherwise identical stimuli, such as encountering other dogs or meeting people, will depend upon which of his territories he happens to be in, this often resulting in Jekyll and Hyde behaviour that many owners find difficult to comprehend, as the pooch who may be quite friendly when coming across another dog in the park can turn into a vicious, snarling beast when faced with the same sort of encounter at home.

The dog's inborn wish to defend its home territory at virtually any cost has of course been put to good use, even exploited, by its human masters. It is one of the reasons why watchdogs are so successful at keeping away would-be intruders: they see every stranger as a trespasser and a threat to their home. Just the same, owners need to recognise that how a dog may behave at home is not by any means how he will comport himself when out in the wider world.

DEEP DOWN HE STILL WANTS TO RUN WITH THE PACK

The second major part of the dog's inherited behaviour are those aspects of it that are the result of it still being a 'pack' animal – just like its wolf predecessors – in the innermost recesses of its psyche, no matter how many tens of thousands of years may have gone by since its ancestors were first domesticated. Even in the meekest 'wouldn't say bow-wow to a goose' lap dogs there runs a deep instinctual – and utterly irreversible – wish to be part of a pack and, ideally, be its leader.

At this point it is worth noting that there are many popular misconceptions about wolves and the way they live in the wild, and it is worthwhile setting the record straight to clear these up. The more you know about wolves, the easier it will be for you to recognise why and how inherited traits manifest themselves in your pet and counteract these as necessary.

To begin with, wolves are not the evil bloodthirsty creatures they're so often portrayed as being in books, films and fairy tales. They are essentially extremely civilised in their behaviour – civilised, that is, if you can see the world from their point of view – demonstrating immense loyalty to their leader and their peers, making utterly devoted and truly caring parents, and generally only killing for food.

Contrary to what the tale of Little Red Riding Hood would have us believe, wolves only rarely attack human beings, generally – and most sensibly – going to great lengths to avoid any contact with humans, well aware that only grief awaits them if the two species were to meet. And on those rare occasions that wolves have attaked humans, this has almost always been because the animals were on the edge of starvation, desperate because they were cornered and fighting for their lives, or were rabid.

What this means as far as your dog is concerned is that it is by no means a ferocious wild animal that is only waiting to resort to its natural instincts before it bites and claws all and sundry. In fact, were a domesticated dog to revert to 'wolfdom', it would probably slink away as it seeks safety away from human contact. In any case, such reversion is not going to happen, because although some 'wolf' is still very much part of your dog's character, much of that underlying trait has been modified by untold generations of evolution and development.

No, should a dog ever become vicious, that will have had little to do with its ancestry, but more than likely will have been the result of 'nurture' rather than 'nature', the animal probably having experienced a mixture of poor training, cruelty and neglect since puppyhood.

HOW A PACK LEADER EMERGES

The other major misconception about wolves is about how they behave in their packs, many people believing that the leader only attains his position after many bloody, even deadly, fights with other contenders. While there may be some fighting at times, the leader figure more commonly emerges after a series of confrontations rather than fights with other hopefuls, these contests being marked more by aggressive body language, snarling and general demonstrations of superiority than by actual violence. Somewhat like dogs that are strangers to each other meeting in a park, a pair of would-be wolf leaders will circle around each other, baring their teeth and making fearsome noises while now and then feinting an attack, until one of them eventually accepts the dominance of the other. Interestingly, just like what happens with a group of dogs, many of the wolves in a pack will not even attempt to seek leadership, quite content to accept as their leader whoever emerges top of any contest (this pragmatic attitude reflecting how those of us who fail to vote in elections will at least pay minimal lip service to the winning party, while still grumbling now and then in the background).

In this you can also can find a parallel with your faithful canine friend, as he too may not seek to overtly contest your leadership, but at the same time will nevertheless now and then have a grumble, this usually taking the form of deliberate disobedience.

Having said that wolves left to their own devices are considerably less violent than depicted by the extremely poor

Press they have received over the ages, it must still be pointed out that occasionally they will fight to the death, such bloody encounters occurring usually because either an outsider – the 'lone wolf' so beloved by fiction – or a member of the pack seeks to overthrow the current leader. You may find echoes of this behaviour in your dog if you introduce another dog – or even a cat – in your home and a contest develops between them.

WHY THERE CAN ONLY BE ONE LEADER

As already touched upon, the territorial imperative is the other major factor in wolf behaviour and this still remains a major motivating force in today's dogs. While it can be desirable for your dog to warn you of intruders by barking (within reason, of course), it is not a good idea for him to start tearing apart visitors from limb to limb, so the extent to which your pooch springs to the defence of what he sees as his fiefdom is something that needs to be carefully kept under control as part of overall training in his early days. Fortunately, most dogs are very quick learners in this respect and will soon learn to match their response to what they perceive as invasions of their territory to one which is more commensurate with the wishes of their leader.

The other essential thing to remember about how instinct governs your dog is that no matter how domesticated he may be, and even though he is the end product of thousand of generations of evolution since his ancestors once were wolves, he will still at heart be a pack animal, and as such will probably when he first joins your household have a go at establishing himself as the leader of his new pack – even if that pack only consists of a human family – and will only ever accept a subordinate role when he learns that this is the only option open to him.

Just as a wolf pack can only have one undisputed leader, your dog's place in the scheme of things in your home has to be made abundantly clear to him: you're the boss, and he is the one who takes orders. Ideally, this all-important message is imparted loudly and clearly to him while he is still a puppy because that indoctrination is going to work best while he is still not too set in his ways. However, in practice, many people acquire dogs that have already reached adulthood and this generally means that they will face more of an uphill task in establishing the vitally important 'I'm the leader, you're the pack' relationship.

Later on in this book – in Chapter 6, How to Talk to Your Dog So He Will Understand You – you will find numerous suggestions and tips that will help you train many aspects of your pet's behaviour, and this information can also be applied in several ways to ensure that you unquestionably become – and always remain – the leader of the pack.

TIPS TO HELP YOU ESTABLISH YOURSELF AS THE LEADER

In the meantime, here are some specific suggestions about how to establish a firm basis for your 'position' in regards to your pet:

❑ At all times, be totally consistent in what you do and do not allow him to do. Sending mixed messages to your dog is just about the worst thing you can do as confusion in his mind is bound to lead to misunderstanding. For example, if you decide that he should not be allowed to get on beds, then never – but never – make exceptions, as a dog's mind cannot sensibly cope with being allowed on the bed in certain circumstances but not in others. Naturally, whatever rules you wish to impose must be equally and consistently applied by other members of your household – all too frequently, a dog will have immense difficulty in coping with a situation where his master forbids him something, but the children allow it.

❑ If you share your home with other humans, decide before

beforehand who will be the dog's *prime* keeper or owner, the person that he will eventually identify as his leader. Ideally, at least during puppyhood, that should also be the person who feeds the dog, because there is an obvious link between being the supplier and dispenser of food and being the master. Naturally, this approach may not always be practical in many circumstances, but even if others than the designated leader have to feed the dog now and then, at least make sure that the leader does it quite frequently.

❑ The same principle should be applied to taking the dog for a walk. Once again, while it may be necessary for other members of the household occasionally to take Fido out for his exercise, most of the time these outings should be under the control of the designated leader. This is particularly important because 'walkies' also provide an ideal opportunity for all kinds of other training, and all these learning experiences should work together to reinforce the basic message of who is the leader.

❑ Never resort to physical punishment to assert your position. If the punishment is at all severe, not only is this to be soundly condemned for humane and ethical reasons, but it will also invariably turn out to be totally counterproductive as instead of instilling respect and loyalty – as well as that all important desire to please you – in your pet it is likely instead to turn him against you, his resentment of previous punishment as well as his fear of similar treatment in the future making him what can only be called a nervous wreck and therefore hardly the best subject for assimilating what you're trying to teach him.

❑ Even if the punishment you mete out is as mild as can be – such as a slap without hardly any force behind it on his rump – that too is unlikely to produce the desired results. A slap that is so gentle that it doesn't cause any discomfort is almost certainly going to be interpreted by your dog as either a friendly, approving pat or even as an invitation to play – in either case, the wrong message is being received and you're only confusing your pet all the more.

❑ Remember that consistent repetition is the key to training any dog, but that any training is going to fall on mainly deaf ears until you have taught him that you're the leader – that is you're the 'one who *must* be obeyed' at all times – as every other aspect of modifying your dog's behaviour will stem from that simple, but at times hard to achieve, inter-relationship.

SPECIAL ASPECTS OF DOMINANCE IN DOGS

Finally, as you might logically expect, it is obviously going to be easier to establish yourself as the master if your dog does not have an overly strong streak of dominance in his character. While some breeds tend to be less dominant by nature than others, even more important is how strongly dominance – that is the inbuilt wish to be the leader – is present in your pet. Naturally, you may not be able to determine this to any great extent if you're acquiring an adult dog because the opportunities to observe his behaviour before committing yourself are likely to be minimal.

However, the situation is quite different when you're choosing a particular puppy from a litter as watching it for a while in the company of its siblings – or even with other dogs – can offer you a golden chance to gauge the extent of its dominance.

Because dominance is a character trait that almost invariably manifests itself very early in a dog, the relative degree to which it is part of the make-up of a particular pup can be determined by watching it carefully when at play with other pups, ideally these coming from the same litter as that way all the pups will have reached more or less the same degree of development and will be just about equal in size.

As you'd expect, dominant puppies are rough and ready

customers; they bounce about, jostling other pups and now and then initiate mock battles by grabbing them by the throat. The other tell-tale sign to watch for is what the pups do when their food is being served – the dominant ones are the first to rush eagerly forward, grabbing all the space and as much food as they can and even snarling to discourage more timid pups who try to join them.

Be aware that you cannot judge the degree to which a dog is dominant by any of the usual yardsticks you might be tempted to think would apply. Neither size nor strength is relevant and the sex of the animal seems to play little role either. So you may well find that a very small elderly female dog can utterly dominate a husky male youngster that belongs to a considerably bigger breed.

When choosing a puppy or a dog, always keep in mind that dominance is a key factor in how readily a pup will respond to and accept training and determines to a very large extent the kind of character he will have when he grows up.

Of course, individual preferences or needs will also play a role in making your final choice – for example, someone wanting a guard dog may value dominance in a dog because it will usually be that much fiercer a defender of its territory, with more submissive animals being more tolerant of intrusion. But, if like most people, you want an easy to get along with dog that is going to try its level best to fit in with your way of life, then choosing one that is not strongly dominant is always going to be your best bet.

But no matter how dominant or submissive your dog may be with other dogs, or even with humans, the one thing that is paramount is that the dominant trait in his character should never be allowed to extend to its owner because, in dog terms, there can only be one boss of his pack and you must ensure that this is you!

Chapter 3
How To Learn Your Dog's Language

As explained previously, the word 'language' does not only encompass the transmission of ideas, emotions and feelings through the use of words, but also includes an exchange of information that is based on what the dictionary calls 'conventional symbols'.

Naturally, what can be considered a 'conventional symbol' will depend greatly on the ability of the 'sender' to express this clearly as well as how skilful the 'receiver' is at interpreting it. Although communication between humans is usually mainly based upon verbalisation, a lot of the information we derive from contact with other people is actually non-verbal. For example, while listening to someone we will automatically at the same time also continuously scan their face and body with our eyes, the expressions we register – usually at a subconscious level – and the changes in the body stance of the speaker all making a major contribution towards improving our perception and understanding of what we're hearing.

There are also numerous examples where conventional symbols replace words in everyday life: the red and green traffic lights that signal stop or go; the icons that have now mainly replaced the words 'Ladies' or 'Gentlemen' on public toilet doors;

and the ubiquitous depiction of a cigarette with a diagonal slash across it to indicate a no smoking area.

In fact, it can be safely argued that the current trend in many areas of inter-human communication is for words to be usurped to a large extent by pictorial representations. And if you have any doubts about that, just take a look at the latest electronic or electrical gadget in your home – where once you might have expected to see words like 'on' and 'off', 'hotter' and 'colder', or 'play' and 'stop', you will nowadays almost certainly find little drawings that illustrate the purpose of a particular knob or control on the device.

In a strange way – although there is much to be said for the everyday practicality of the use of almost universally understood icons – the spread of 'talking through pictures' can also be seen as a retrograde step, a sort of insidious dumbing down of language.

Whatever may be the merits of that point of view, and no matter how content we may or not be to receive information from other humans through visual symbols, many of us tend to forget that, apart from the odd monosyllabic grunt or groan, 'signs' and 'symbols' were the first means of communication between our ancestors when man first appeared on the scene.

And it serves us well to remember how we first 'talked' to each other when we set out to learn the language of our dogs, as it in many ways has strong parallels with man's early attempts to achieve a meaningful exchange of information with others of his kind.

Rather like primitive man, today's domestic dogs rely mainly on relatively few sounds and a great deal of symbols to 'talk', both among themselves and to us.

Because humans are extremely good at expressing themselves through a wide variety of sounds and have an immensely rich spoken vocabulary, we tend to fall into the trap of considering verbal signals the most important method of communication even when we are trying to establish meaningful contact with other species, failing to pay sufficient attention to other forms of 'talk'. If there is one thing you can do to begin to increase your understanding of dog talk, it is to set aside this natural preference for sound-based talk and start to accord much more attention to all the other signals our dogs are constantly sending us. Keeping that in mind, there now follow hints and suggestions on how to make your understanding of what your dog is telling you more effective and turn you into a better pupil of his language.

SETTING OUT TO LEARN DOG TALK

Learning dog language is a very different experience from acquiring another human language that is foreign to you. To begin with, in many instances, such as an English-speaking person learning, say, Dutch or Spanish, you will have the advantage that even before you start you will already know – or be to able to accurately guess – the meaning of many words in the language you're learning. For example, when the Dutch say 'huis' or the Germans 'haus', it will be a pretty safe bet that 'house' is likely to be the English equivalent.

In fact, you may be surprised that even if you never learned French, you already know something like one in ten of its words (just about all words ending in 'on', such as 'companion', 'decision' or 'comparison' mean the same in both languages, although the pronunciation will be somewhat different).

Apart from the immediate benefit conferred by any already shared vocabulary, the other thing that will stand you in good stead when coming to grips with another human language is that in most instances you will also already have a pretty good insight into its *syntax* – a word that describes the totality of facts about the grammatical arrangement of words in a language – as well as be able to at times form a reasonably accurate impression of what is being discussed by the context of the situation, this providing often a pretty good clue as to what otherwise incomprehensible words may mean.

Unfortunately, when it comes to dog talk, all of these advantages are lost, because what your pooch may be saying in its own way bears little – if any – resemblance to anything that is part of inter-human communication methods. Yet, strange though it may seem, you don't actually have to start from scratch, because, somewhat like people knowing more French words than they are aware of, you will almost certainly already have had some basic grounding in dog talk. Depending upon your circumstances, such dog talk as you already recognise if not always understand may have come from your dog – or dogs you or your family previously owned – as well as the many depictions of dogs you will have seen during your lifetime in illustrations, movies and cartoon strips. Generally, you will not be consciously aware of the accumulation of information about dog talk that you will have stored in your mind over the years, but stored it will have been, and it will take minimal effort to retrieve it so it can be put to good use as you strive to increase your understanding of your dog.

Indeed, it can be safely said that just about everybody will already have a substantial fund of knowledge that will ease their efforts to decipher what their dog is telling them. And, if you doubt that statement, consider for a moment how many people do you think there might be in the world that do not instinctively know that it's a good idea to give a wide berth to a snarling dog who has his teeth bared?

LISTEN TO YOUR DOG: HIS MESSAGE MAY BE A LIFESAVER

While you doubtlessly already have your very own good reasons for wanting to learn dog talk – if you didn't you probably wouldn't be reading this — a greater awareness of what your four-legged friend is telling you may even possibly save your life.

While that claim may at first seem somewhat over the top, you only have to make the most cursory of searches of the Internet to find almost countless accounts of instances where the household pet alerted his human family to impending danger and so literally saved them from death or injury. Impending earthquakes, ravaging floods, devastating cyclones and tornadoes, these are but a few of the natural disasters that dogs seem to be able to sense beforehand — and when they do, there will invariably be changes in their behaviour, changes that an observant owner would do well to take notice of.

Usually, a dog will send his 'disaster of some kind is pending' message' through behaviour that is quite out of keeping with his normal demeanour, but the exact form of his altered conduct will vary greatly according to how he was brought up. While it will be your pet's natural inclination to warn you of something bad about to happen through urgent and excited barking, he may be inhibited from doing this because you've trained him never to bark, so he may instead circle excitedly around you or keep jumping up and down.

However, whatever form any unusual behaviour by your pet may take, it is something that should never be ignored or casually dismissed as 'Oh, it's just Rover acting the silly fool again' because, as numerous accounts bear witness, the chances are high that he will be trying to tell you something really important – be that an overboiling saucepan in the kitchen, an intruder on your premises, or even a fire that is smouldering in an upstairs bedroom.

Incidentally, although this may seem pretty obvious, before you can identify highly unusual behaviour by your dog, you first have to know what his normal patterns are – one more good reason why it pays to spend time observing your dog carefully during various activities.

This last observation naturally sets the scene for specific guidelines that will assist you as you prepare to learn your dog's language.

THE THREE STAGES OF LEARNING DOG TALK

To put it in the proverbial nutshell, there are three key steps that when applied together will enable you to quickly and accurately pick up your dog's vocabulary:

1.   Careful observation of your dog's behaviour; and
2.   Memorising what you've observed; and
3.   Interpreting what you've observed and memorised.

That, you're almost bound to say, seems logical, simple and straightforward enough. So it is, but each of these inter-dependent steps does deserve a fuller explanation to ensure that you get the maximum benefit in the quickest possible time when you apply them.

OBSERVATION

If we refer once again to our faithful Collins English Dictionary, we will find that one of the definitions, the one that matters to us in this context, for the word 'observation' is the 'detailed examination of phenomena prior to analysis, diagnosis, or interpretation', and that could hardly have been put better or more concisely, but for our purposes some specific elaboration is still necessary.

To begin with, please note that the process of observing something must invariably begin with a 'detailed examination' of whatever it is that we're observing. In other words, successful observation will not result from now and then casually glancing at whatever your dog may be up to at the moment. How your dog acts and reacts under various circumstances – has to be examined in some detail before your research can bear fruit.

Here are some tips to help you achieve that detailed examination so that it eventually covers the gamut of your dog's activities:

❑ Whenever your dog is with you, make sure that you not only register the obvious outward signs of his behaviour, such as whether he's running, sitting, barking, or whatever, but also deliberately pay attention to details that may be less obvious, such as small, almost imperceptible changes in the positioning of his ears and tail, and also including whether he is making any sounds whose volume is so low that you wouldn't otherwise hear them unless you strove to perceive them, or whether his eyes and the rest of his face alter in expression.

❑ Mentally note not only your dog's current behaviour in response to whatever stimulus may be present, but also try to relate what he is doing at the time to whatever activities immediately preceded his present ones, as well as taking into account what he does next. Much of the time, a dog's behaviour at a given moment is not an isolated event but is part of a sequence of several changes in behaviour that together may span several minutes and extend backward – as well as eventually forward – in time. It follows from this that a 'snapshot' observation that only records a brief moment in time is not likely to be as valuable an aid to interpretation as one that covers a longer period.

❑ Another important aspect to consider is the context of the situation in which your dog is producing various patterns of behaviour. Seemingly similar behaviour – such as his tail wagging freely and vigorously – may well be indications of quite different underlying emotional states, the exact nature of which can depend upon whether his tail starts to wag when you're dishing out his favourite food in the kitchen or whether the wagging occurs as he's being approached by a human who is a stranger to him in the park.

❑ It is also equally important to remain aware that your dog may be responding to other stimuli reasonably nearby as you observe his behaviour. For example, should his nose start to twitch while you're playing with him in your living room, that twitching may have nothing whatsoever to do with the activity at hand but may be his response to cooking smells emanating from a neighbour's kitchen, smells so faint that you can't perceive them but he can.

MEMORISATION

No matter how detailed your observation of various aspects of your dog's behaviour may be, it will serve little purpose if you can't remember accurately or fully enough some time later what you've seen.

Memory can be a tricky thing, especially when you're using it to store a variety of impressions in a short time. Two tips to ensure better recall of your dog's patterns of behaviour:

❑ Although some might think of this as using a sledgehammer to crack a nut, there is nothing quite like a few written notes to jog your memory, and it can be immensely helpful to jot down a few words after you've spent some time observing your dog. These notes don't have to be all that complete, providing they cover the salient points and are clear enough that you won't have any difficulty deciphering them some time later. Generally, only a few words will serve admirably for this purpose, such as 'got up from the floor, circled the room a few times, gave a small almost inaudible bark and headed for the front door – two minutes the children arrived home from school'. Or 'didn't seem to want to settle as usual in his favourite spot in the living room after having been fed; but instead kept wandering around, his nose close to the carpet' – the likely explanation discovered later: he had accidentally tipped over his food bowl in the kitchen'.

❏ While you will often be able to ascribe almost immediately a cause in many instances to a particular behaviour, such as in the examples cited directly above, at other times the reason for your dog's demeanour may be considerably less obvious. However, if you keep a note of what you've seen on several previous occasions, you may well find that previously elusive answers suddenly become crystal clear as you review your jottings at leisure some time later.

INTERPRETATION

This last step is, of course, the most important of the three, because this is when you get to finally apply everything you have learned along the way to definite practical purposes and this is also when, all being well, you start to truly reap all the benefits of your previous efforts.

By the way, it should perhaps be mentioned first at this point that although the three steps involved in the overall process of observation, memorising and interpreting need to follow each other sequentially for any particular aspect of your dog's behaviour, you certainly do not need to wait until you've completed *all* your observations and memorised them before you can begin to interpret your findings.

Any time you believe you have enough information on hand to interpret and give meaning to a particular kind of behaviour, do go ahead and start drawing your conclusions. In fact, interpreting as you go along instead of trying to do this all at the end of the exercise can be extremely helpful because you will have the benefit of what you've already learned to make it easier to understand additional patterns of behaviour. As it is with so many things, a bit of practice in your interpretation methods is likely to affect these for the better.

While, as has been stated, there is no good reason why you shouldn't interpret what your dog is telling you one bit at a time, it can be most worthwhile and instructive to review conclusions you had reached earlier when you've accumulated more knowledge and probably have a better insight into your dog's way of thinking and expressing himself. You may well discover quite frequently that at least some of your original interpretations will need to be adjusted in the light of your increased experience. This, of course, is one more good reason why you should keep reasonably detailed notes as part of the memorising step as these will help you review earlier findings.

Like learning any new skill, the process of acquiring dog talk can seem daunting at first. But, as is the case with so many other tasks, this one gets easier the more you practise it.

Truthfully, as will be explained further in the next chapter, the way your dog talks is really not all that difficult to decipher, providing you take the time first to acquire some canine 'vocabulary' and then apply this using the approach outlined above, to the very specific and personal ways your dog expresses himself.

Chapter 4

A Basic Guide To Everyday Dog Talk

As we've discovered in previous chapters, our dogs 'talk' to us in many different ways in addition to the sounds they produce.

While you, of course, will be mainly interested in how your own pet expresses himself, all dogs initially share a common language. Often there are variations in the exact form this takes in individuals, as a puppy's original vocabulary is modified and enlarged as he grows up. At a practical level this means that while you can expect your dog to express himself *broadly* in the same way as other dogs, you must also take into account that it 'ain't always necessarily so'.

Nevertheless, despite these possible differences, there will be enough common factors between how your pet communicates with others around him and how his brethren do, to make the following basic guide to what can be called 'everyday' dog talk pretty accurate most of the time.

Going on from there, let's begin by listing the main ways through which dogs express themselves in a manner that humans can discern. These are as follows, although not necessarily listed here in order of importance because the importance of a particular means of expression will vary according to what is being expressed:

❑ The overall body positioning.
❑ The positioning of the ears.
❑ The expression in the eyes.
❑ The positioning of the jaw.
❑ The positioning of the tail.
❑ The production of sounds.

In addition to those listed above, there are several other indicators that can reflect a dog's state of mind and emotions, but which are not always all that apparent. For example, most of us are aware that when the hairs on the neck, the shoulders, and/or the back of a dog near where its tail begins – these hairs collectively known as the 'hackles' – rise, this almost certainly means that the animal is either angry or afraid. However, though the rise of the hackles will usually convey an important warning, with some breeds of dogs – such as those that are extremely short-haired or virtually bald – the hackles may rise but not enough that this can be readily seen.

Of course, the correct interpretation of your dog's messages almost never relies only upon one behavioural aspect. Usually, there will be several indicators that have to be considered together to arrive at the proper conclusion.

The range of emotions and feelings that your dog can convey through body language and sound is quite vast, but the majority of these can be placed in one of the eight principal categories that are now described in some detail, together with illustrations.

AGGRESSION – THE WARNING SIGNALS

It can, of course, be of the greatest importance to be able to recognise aggressive behaviour, and do so long before it actually turns into any kind of violence that puts either other animals or people at risk of attack.

Fortunately, true innate aggression in dogs is comparatively rare. Aggressive behaviour – or the prelude to it – is in most cases the result of the dog having either been provoked to some substantial extent or of the animal being scared by circumstances that it doesn't understand, causing it – almost as a last resort – to choose 'fight' rather than 'flight'.

While a dog may suddenly spring into 'attack mode', this will more commonly be preceded by a host of warning signals that this is about to happen unless the situation changes quickly.

Typical indications that warn of the likelihood of aggressive behaviour include:

❑ The dog stands stiffly, and its legs and most of its body are rigid, almost as though he is frozen in place.

❑ The animal pins back his ears, drawing them close to the sides of his head (it does this so that his delicate ears will present a smaller target should a fight ensue). However, the ears may be upright immediately before any attack (to improve hearing), to then flatten just as the attack takes place.

❑ The dog stares intently with eyes that are narrowed; at times his pupils will be fully dilated. He may also turn his head somewhat to the side while still staring with great intensity towards his target (this positioning of the face is known as 'giving whole eye' because it makes the whites of a dog's eyes appear bigger, so presenting a more fearsome appearance).

❑ The tail is likely to be stretched straight out to its fullest length.

❑ The jaws are likely to be partly open with the lips pulled back in a snarl.

❑ Usually, intermittent growling that emanates from deep down the dog's throat will also accompany aggressive or hostile behaviour.

In *behaviour typical of potential aggression, he's giving the 'whole eye' look, and has also adopted a stance that makes him appear bigger and more ferocious than he really is.*

This dog is eager to attack his target as he strains at his leash, his ears pinned back and his gaze intent.

There is no mistaking the signals of aggression this dog is transmitting: the jaws are open in a snarl, ready to bite; the gaze is intently fixed; and the hairs on the back of his neck are raised.

FEAR – A FREQUENT PRECURSOR TO AGGRESSION

While most of the behaviour that indicates aggression in a dog is pretty obvious even to the least knowledgeable of observers, some of the key signals that indicate fear – which, of course, is frequently a precursor to aggression – can be more subtle and may not immediately be recognised, especially if only a few of them are present.

Typical signs of fear include:

❑ The dog's whole body adopts a lowered stance, almost as though his legs have shrunk (the purpose of this behaviour is so that he will present a smaller, less vulnerable target to any would-be attacker).

❑ The dog will probably be looking away from whatever it is that is arousing his fear, or, alternatively, may be moving his head in a to and fro sideways movement.

❏ As with aggression, the hackles may rise.

❏ Usually, the tail will be well down and tucked closely against the dog's hindquarters, and it may be either motionless in that position or be wagging frantically.

❏ The 'whole eye' look, already described above, may also be evident, and the pupils will usually be dilated.

❏ Fear is also often marked by sporadic barks, these intensifying in volume and frequency if the dog becomes increasingly apprehensive.

This dog is showing several of the signs that indicate fearfulness. Obviously, he is extremely unsure of the situation that faces him and, accordingly, he has adopted a lowered stance by partly bending his legs and arching his spine, moved his ears against his head, and brought his tail down, readying it to be tucked away underneath him.

Deeply worried if not yet downright fearful, this pup has sought refuge under his master's leg. Even tucked away in what he thinks is a safer place, he displays some of the typical signs that indicate fear: his ears are down, his back and head are lowered; and his intent look is marked by unusually dilated pupils.

CONFIDENCE – THE SIGNALS THAT SPELL SELF-ASSURANCE

Confidence in a dog stems from two separate yet connected sources. First, there is the natural confidence he has in himself and his ability to deal successfully with anything that might come his way, the level of this confidence varying greatly according to the dog's natural character, his breed, and how he was brought up. Secondly, there is the confidence that results from the trust he places in his master and, by extension, other members of his human family.

Generally speaking, a confident dog is also a happy dog, one that is aware of his place in the universe and mostly expects good rather than bad things to come his way.

Typical signs of confidence include:

- ❏ Whether standing still or walking, the dog will adopt a naturally erect stance, neither striving to make himself look bigger or smaller than he is.

- ❏ His facial expression will be relaxed with his gaze being attentive but not intent and his pupils will be quite small.

- ❏ His jaws will be either just about closed, or partly open if that's required to aid perspiration (most of which occurs through his tongue which therefore needs ventilation).

- ❏ The ears may be either pricked up to their maximum height or pricked forward or just loosely hanging down (this hanging down is quite different from the pinning back of the ears that can indicate either aggression or fear).

- ❏ The tail will generally be up in the air and most likely to be moving in a series of slow sideways sweeps.

The typical pose of a truly confident dog who has no doubts about his position in the world and almost certainly holds himself in extremely high esteem, considering himself to be a true prince amongst dogs. Note how the facial expression is relaxed, the jaws slightly open but hanging slackly, and the ears are 'at ease'.

Confidence just oozes from this puppy, as it stands totally relaxed, looking directly but not intently at whatever catches his attention, with his tail upright but curling towards his back.

DOMINANCE – THE EVER-PRESENT DESIRE TO BE TOP DOG

As we have seen in previous chapters, most dogs have an extremely strong wish to be the leader of their pack. It is to be hoped that somewhere along the way during his upbringing you have disabused your pet of the very idea that anyone else but you could be the master, and that he has accepted his subordinate position fully and cheerfully.

However, although your dog may never again try to contest your leadership, this does not mean that he has abandoned any hopes of dominating other dogs, thereby still making him a leader of sorts. This inborn wish to be in charge, to be – to use a phrase that is particularly apt in this context – the 'top dog', runs so deeply in the psychological makeup of most dogs that it is hardly ever fully eradicated. Just because he has failed in his attempt to dominate his human master doesn't mean that your dog is prepared to abandon completely his desire to be in control of other situations, more specifically those involving other dogs.

It is indeed when he is in the company of other dogs that your pet is most likely to exhibit the typical behavioural traits of dominance, which include:

❑ When in a dominant mood, your pet will stand tall, his legs fully erect so that the height he gains may provide him with an advantage in regard to smaller, shorter dogs.

❑ Given the opportunity, your dog will attempt to stand directly above another dog, literally looking down on him.

❑ To demonstrate clearly who holds the upper hand (or should that be 'paw'?) your dog may attempt to place his paw, or at times his chin, over the other dog's shoulder.

❑ Mounting another dog from behind – or attempting this – is another classical sign of dominance, although at times, and rather paradoxically, this can also be the way that a subordinate dog demonstrates his status to one that ranks higher.

In a clear expression of his dominant status, the bigger dog has placed his paw on the shoulder of the smaller one.

SUBMISSION – THE ACCEPTANCE OF A SUBORDINATE ROLE

Submissiveness is, of course, the other side of the dominance coin, and you will usually have an opportunity to see both of these behaviours at the same time when two or more dogs are playing together.

Typical signs of submission include:

❑ The dog will stand with both his head and body lowered.

❑ He will not resist attempts by dominant playmates to hook their paw or chin over his shoulders or back, but will meekly acquiesce without any protest.

❑ The submissive dog will have a tendency to look away from other dogs, avoiding direct eye contact.

❑ The lower-ranking dog will often express his acceptance of his subordinate status by licking tentatively at the lips and the corners of the mouth of the one he sees as his superior.

❑ As a sign of total submission, the lower-ranking dog may roll on to his back, his head well out of the way, offering his chest and abdomen in deliberate total vulnerability.

❑ The tail of the submissive dog will usually be well down, at times even tucked away between his legs.

There's no mistaking the signals sent out by these two dogs – the supine dog is clearly saying to the bigger one, 'I accept that I am your subordinate, and therefore I will not try to fight you, but instead offer you total and utter surrender.'

STRESS AND ANXIETY – WHEN IT'S ALL TOO MUCH FOR YOUR DOG

There are, of course, many different kinds of stress – mental, emotional and physical, to name but the three main categories – but they all essentially mean that the subject is suffering from some form of undue pressure he cannot cope with easily or comfortably.

However, no matter what may be the underlying cause of your dog's stress, the typical signals of it include:

❑ The eyes will appear disorientated and will exhibit a glazed appearance with fully dilated pupils. The dog will also usually seek to avoid direct eye contact, turning his head away. There may also be a higher than usual rate of blinking.

❑ Yawning and the nervous licking of lips or the nose are often early signs of an increasing stress level.

❑ There may also be behaviour that hints at disorientation, such as random but intense sniffing, sporadic scratching, and shaking that resembles that which a dog does to clear the water from his body after he has had a bath or been swimming.

❑ If the stress level is more than just moderate the dog will generally whine intermittently, the whines being usually accompanied by panting or rapid breathing.

In most cases, stress will be marked by several of the signs mentioned above, a collection of such signs being known as a 'cluster'. How you deal with the situation will depend upon whether you can identify and remove or ease the cause of the stress – for example, it may be due to other dogs nearby or the result of your dog suffering from exposure to too much heat, in which case the remedies will be obvious enough. However, if there is no discernible reason why your dog should be stressed and the signs of it fail to abate within a reasonable time, you should consult a vet because various ailments and illnesses can also trigger this behaviour.

The panting tongue, the glassy-eyed look and the general air of disorientation all indicate that this is a dog who is pretty stressed out.

CALMING SIGNALS THAT TAKE OFF THE PRESSURE

A great deal of the stress that dogs suffer comes, as might be expected, from other dogs, much of it stemming from their inheritance of various forms of pack behaviour. This pack behaviour can at times place great pressure upon dogs who are less than certain about their place in the hierarchy.

Whenever dog meets dog, there will always be an element of contest involved, this at its highest when the dogs are complete strangers but even still present to some extent when they already know each other quite well. Signs indicating dominance and/or submissiveness will be exchanged between the dogs when they meet. These signs, when the dogs are already acquainted, usually only serve to reinforce and re-establish a previously agreed pecking order.

As part of that process, dogs will also send out what are known as 'calming signals', forms of behaviour that are aimed at easing the situation and reducing any risk of conflict. A calming signal is not the same as an indication of submissiveness, but in effect says 'Hey, big boy, take it easy, there's no need to look for trouble. We're all members of the same pack, and, what's more, you and I are fully aware of our respective places in the greater scheme of things.'

While your dog will primarily use calming signals for the benefit of other dogs, he may also present one or more of these when dealing with humans, such as, for example, when he feels he may have done something wrong and is, as it were, 'in the doghouse'.

Typical calming signals – whether directed at other dogs or humans – include:

- The dog looks away, avoiding direct eye contact.

- He may act as though he is distracted by other, more intriguing things, hoping that his obvious lack of interest in the current situation will diffuse any possible confrontation.

- His feigned disinterest is also likely to be manifested by wandering around or circling in a seemingly aimless manner, perhaps stopping frequently to sniff the ground intently, or by simply sitting or lying down to indicate his total lack of enthusiasm to participate in any kind of contest.

- Although as already mentioned earlier, a dog's licking of his nose and lips can indicate other emotional states, this behaviour is also used frequently as a calming signal that more or less says, 'I'm no threat to you; I'm too busy attending to other things.'

This puppy is licking his nose, one of the many stylised ways that dogs can send calming signals to each other when a confrontation may be looming.

Wandering around in a circle with little obvious purpose, stopping now and then to sniff the ground, this dog is transmitting a strong calming signal that tells other dogs that he is no threat to them in any way.

PLAYFUL INVITATIONS

At a casual glance, much of the behaviour that dogs exhibit during play with other dogs or with humans seems rather similar to that which accompanies attempts to establish dominance. A closer look will, however, reveal substantial differences: the dogs' whole demeanour will be considerably more relaxed, and their intention to play rather than fight will usually have been announced beforehand with some ritualised behaviour that signals loudly and clearly that they want to have fun.

Typical examples of behaviour that mark play or which are invitations to play include:

❑ The so-called 'play bow', which is performed to get the play started. This most descriptive phrase denotes the stylised little dance that dogs tend to do when they want to play, leaning forward on their front paws and then bounding away to return and 'bow' once again. The play bow is used both with other dogs and with humans.

- ❑ Another standard invitation to play takes the form of the dog sitting on its haunches and then repeatedly pawing the air with one of its forelegs.

- ❑ Alternatively, the dog may stretch its front legs in front of itself, raise its hindquarters and produce short and soft barking sounds in expectation of the excitement to come.

- ❑ While play – especially if it becomes rough play – may be accompanied by barking, the barks will be at a higher pitch than when they express aggression or fear.

- ❑ Another aspect of play behaviour that is often misinterpreted is when dogs attempt to mount each other, but in this context this doesn't have any sexual connotations nor is it a way of expressing dominance.

- ❑ Even during the roughest of play, dogs will remain fairly relaxed about it, although it may seem otherwise to a human observer. One key sign to watch out for is whether the dog's lips hang loosely to cover his teeth or whether the mouth is drawn back in the snarl that typically signals aggression.

'Please play with me!' The play bow is your dog's cheerful invitation for someone to join him for some fun and games.

It may look like fierce fighting, but these dogs are just engaged in some rough play. To distinguish the difference between the two behaviours, look at how relaxed both dogs are as they engage in a bit of frolicsome rough-house and especially note that although the dogs' teeth are visible their lips are not drawn in a snarl.

In this illustrated guide, we have covered the main emotional states that are reflected by 'normal' dog behaviour. While this basic insight will go a long way towards helping you understand the many and varied signals your dog is always sending out as he 'talks' to you, the meaning of more unusual behaviour will be explained in the next chapter.

Chapter 5

Hints For Understanding What Your Dog Is Telling You

Although the principal aspects of how dogs act in response to their most common 'mainstream' emotional states have been fully described in the previous chapter, there are many additional ways through which our dogs 'talk' to us.

In this chapter, you will find information to help you understand some of the more unusual – and even abnormal – behavioural patterns that dogs may present at times, and there will also be some extra notes about their 'language'.

To begin with, it's worth taking a brief look at how various forms of animal behaviours are classified, these classifications applying most specifically to dogs. Essentially, behavioural patterns can be divided into four main groups:

❑ Normal behaviour
❑ Abnormal behaviour
❑ Pathological behaviour
❑ Allelomimetic behaviour

Let's now look at these groups in some detail.

NORMAL BEHAVIOUR

Normal behaviour, as you might have guessed, is behaviour that is, well 'normal', and which is broadly within what might have been expected.

Simple though that definition appears on the surface, it does need to be pointed out that in context 'normal' means what is the 'average' behaviour of a specific species and breed, as well as this being related to a given geographical area and also to a period of time.

In other words, what is considered normal for dogs will depend upon all of these variables. What is normal for an Alsatian may be not be so for a Dachshund and 'normalcy' will also be affected by whether the dog is a fully domesticated family pet or is pulling sleds in Alaska. And while it may be intriguing to study how dogs lived in Biblical times, this may not always be enlightening when you're considering how best to convince Rover that curtains aren't vertical chewing toys.

ABNORMAL BEHAVIOUR

At its simplest, 'abnormal' behaviour is defined as that which to some *substantial* extent differs from that which is considered as normal.

The key word in that definition is 'substantial' and that's the part of the phrase experts can argue about forever. Exactly how great must deviations in behaviour be to be deemed as 'substantial'? And can occasional or rare variations from the norm ever be seen as 'substantial'? And how much latitude in behaviour do you allow for the simple fact that dogs, like humans, are after all individuals and therefore cannot be expected to behave identically.

Again as with humans, the fine line that separates normal and abnormal behaviour can all too often be blurred. Accordingly, never be in too great a hurry to judge some highly individualistic aspect of your dog's behaviour as being abnormal, as it is more likely to be just an idiosyncratic characteristic resulting from his upbringing.

PATHOLOGICAL BEHAVIOUR

While it can often be difficult to distinguish between normal and abnormal behaviour, there is a fairly simple test to identify what can safely be called pathological behaviour – the word 'pathological', of course, meaning 'related to, involved with, or caused by disease'.

To apply this test, ask yourself a simple question: is the somewhat unusual behaviour you're concerned with merely an *exaggerated* form of normal behaviour or is it behaviour that is so over the top that the extent to which it differs from the norm puts it in an altogether different class? If your answer to this is that the behaviour is merely exaggerated, then it's almost certainly merely abnormal; however, should you conclude that what you've observed goes well beyond exaggeration, then it's most likely that the behaviour is truly pathological in origin.

It can be truly vital to be able to accurately make the distinction between what is and isn't pathological behaviour. Your conclusion will dictate what remedies are likely to be suitable, because, while most abnormal behaviour can usually be corrected or controlled by usual training methods, evidence of genuinely pathological behaviour almost certainly means that you should consult a vet so that any underlying condition can be diagnosed and treated.

ALLELOMIMETRIC BEHAVIOUR

Dogs now and then can develop unusual behaviour that doesn't neatly fall into any of the categories already mentioned and for which there is no apparent explanation. In some instances this can be a manifestation of *allelomimetric* behaviour, this being defined as behaviour that influences another to emulate it.

This copycat – or should that be 'copydog'? – response, while common to many other species – is particularly likely to occur in dogs, mainly because their wolf ancestors lived together as packs and therefore were wont to imitate each other so as to blend in better with their fellow pack members.

A typical example of allelomimetric behaviour – and one which many dog owners will have experienced to their chagrin – is when your normally quiet pet starts to howl just because a neighbouring dog is baying at the moon. In this instance, your dog's howling will not be in response to the same stimulus that started off the neighbour's dog – that is the moon – but will instead be a reaction to the other dog's howling.

Another typical example of this type of behaviour is when several dogs are playing together and one of them runs off for whatever reason, to be immediately followed by the rest of them. What is actually happening here is not just a bunch of dogs playing follow the leader but a clear demonstration of allelomimetric behaviour that has its roots all the way back in time in the dogs' inherited instinctual traits.

While such contagious behaviour usually confers little, if any, benefit to today's domestic dogs, it was an invaluable aid to survival for their ancestors, because it meant that if one member of a pack of wolves decided to make a run for it to escape sensed danger, the remainder would follow suit and also escape to safety. Equally, this behaviour also helped wolves hunt as a pack, because when one went after prey the others automatically joined in, their numbers increasing their chances of success. Incidentally, the so-called 'herd instinct' that is so marked in cows, sheep and horses is but another manifestation of this ancient behavioural trait.

Applying the above to an everyday practical level, this means that when you can't make rhyme or reason out of some aspect of how your dog behaves, you may find the answer by considering whether the behaviour that mystifies you is due to him copying the actions of another dog.

TREMBLING AND SHIVERING

It's not all that uncommon for a dog to become a quivering jelly in a corner of the room for five or ten minutes. Dogs tremble – or more accurately, shiver – for a number of possible reasons that can be divided roughly into two main classifications:

❑ Emotion-induced shivers that are usually brought on by the dog being either excited or frightened; and

❑ Shivering that is the direct result of an underlying physical cause, such as the dog is simply cold or may be running a fever.

If your pet is in a good state of overall health, then it's almost certain that any trembling will be a symptom of what might be called an 'emotional overload' when, for whatever reason, he becomes over-excited.

As already suggested previously, it will often be possible for you to determine what triggers off this behaviour, as the source of the dog's concern may be quite obvious. At other times, however, there may be no apparent reason for either trembling or shivering. In these instances, you may well be able to identify the root cause of the behaviour by making a careful note of what events preceded the shivers or, perhaps just as likely, what events your dog may be anticipating. For example, do the shivers usually occur some time before his walk is due? Or do they follow a period of intensive play in the garden? Or has your dog just seen a bird through the window? All of these 'triggers' have been noted by dog owners as setting off shivering in their pets.

Once you've discovered what trigger mechanisms affect your dog, you can thereafter probably reduce the frequency of shivering episodes by making a suitable alteration in his lifestyle. In relation to the examples mentioned above this might be accomplished by varying the timing of the walks, stopping playtime well before over-excitement sets in, and perhaps keeping the curtains partly drawn.

While most shivering dogs are simply over-excited, it must also be stressed that shivering or trembling that continues unabated for more than, say, half an hour or so could be a symptom of sickness and if this happens the dog should be seen by a vet without undue delay.

PREVENTING DOG BITES

The typical signs of aggressive behaviour have already been described earlier. However, because aggression can at times lead to an attack on a human and possibly result in someone being bitten, there now follow guidelines that can help you avoid this happening.

❑ When you're approaching a dog to which you're a stranger, do so by moving closer to one of its sides, rather than head on. While most humans tend to approach a dog head on and probably lean down towards him, this behaviour will be perceived by the dog as a threat. If the dog is already in the slightest bit nervous, he is likely to react aggressively. However, a dog will perceive an approach towards one of his sides as at best being friendly in nature, but at the worst as neutral.

❑ If a dog is particularly nervous, it's usually best to leave him alone. However, if for some overwhelming reason you absolutely must get near to him (as when you're trying to read the information on his collar because you think he may be lost), gain his confidence by first squatting down a few feet away from him, your back turned towards him. Hold this pose for a couple of minutes or so before you gently and slowly turn around and then try to approach one of his sides.

❑ Should the dog cower away from you – or, even worse, actually snap or growl at you – don't ever move closer in an attempt to pacify him, as this will only make him feel even more intimidated and, accordingly, raise his aggression level.

❑ If the circumstances are such that, having safely approached the dog, you need to grab him by the collar, always do so with extreme caution because it is a statistical fact that something like 25 per cent of all dog bites occurred as the animal's collar was being grasped.

SPECIAL SAFETY TIPS FOR PARENTS

While children and dogs sometimes seem as though they were meant for each other, there is always a very real danger that when they play or mix together the child may be bitten. One particularly worrying aspect about dog bites is that most of them occur within the owner's premises and that nearly half of them involve children being bitten by the family pet.

Bark Busters, the world's largest dog training company, has compiled a set of helpful guidelines for parents that can reduce the risk of children being bitten by strange or familiar dogs. Their recommendations (with some additional notes from other sources) are:

❑ Under no circumstances should a baby ever be left alone with any dog, including the faithful family pet you've had for years and who has never shown any kind of aggressive behaviour in his life.

❑ Young children should never be allowed to walk or feed a dog unsupervised, as the risk of unusual behaviour is always greater during these activities.

❑ Never allow a small child to discipline a dog because the dog may well respond in an unexpected, possibly dangerous, way.

❑ Never allow children to pull on a dog's collar or engage in aggressive or rough play with it.

❑ As a general rule, children should be taught to never pet a strange dog, no matter how friendly he may appear, even if the owner is present.

❑ Children should be taught to stay away from dogs – including family pets – that are eating or sleeping, and avoid dogs that have new puppies.

❑ Dogs that are tied up should never be approached; and, in keeping with this, children should never be allowed to retrieve a ball or other toys from an unfamiliar garden.

❑ The whole family should be trained in the various forms of communication behaviour that stem from a dog's 'pack' heritage, and, in particular, should also be taught how to make a dog react submissively through use of correct body language and voice control.

Naturally, it is not only children who get bitten by dogs, as many adults suffer the same fate. To reduce the risk of being bitten, Bark Busters offers these additional safety tips about what to do when a dog approaches you:

❑ Don't try to make friends with an unfamiliar dog.

❑ Stand still, stand tall and don't move a muscle until the dog loses interest in you – don't try to run away.

❑ Allow the dog to smell you but don't put your hand out; let the dog come close to you on its own terms. Dogs will often conduct multiple 'tests' to determine whether a stranger is friend, foe or neutral, and it is during these that some problems may occur, so remember to stay alert.

❑ Face the dog at all times but don't make direct eye contact with the dog or stare at it, as this can be perceived as a sign of aggression.

❑ To extricate yourself from a risky situation, back away slowly, watching the dog from the corner of your eye.

❑ If the dog knocks you down, roll up into a foetal position with your arms covering your head and neck and play dead; don't fight back. However, do not roll up like this just because you *feel* threatened; as that could actually incite an attack. Follow these instructions only if you have been knocked down.

SOME ADDITIONAL NOTES ABOUT BARKING

In the previous chapter that dealt with various emotional states, barking was already mentioned several times. Just the same, barking is such a vast subject that some additional notes are in order, including providing answers to those two most frequently asked questions: How many different kinds of barking are there? And does the same kind of bark always mean the same thing?

All barking sounds can be roughly classified as belonging to one of three main groups, according to the emotion that provokes them: excitement, fear, and warning. Additionally, there is also whining, which while not strictly the same as barking, is nevertheless a form of vocal communication as are baying and howling.

Speaking generally, a specific type of bark will always mean the same thing, no matter what breed the dog belongs to, although the amount of barking you can expect from a dog will vary considerably from breed to breed, ranging from the

Greyhound's almost permanent silence to the Chihuahua's virtually constant vocalisation of its feelings. And, apart from the breed differences, the frequency of barking also varies considerably among individual dogs. As a rule of thumb, the more excitable the dog, the more he will bark.

The barking messages aren't hard to decipher: the growling bark that comes from deep within the throat is clearly a warning signal; the high-pitched bark that accompanies a favourite game is an expression of joy and delight; the whining of pups, usually when they're feeling cold or lonely, is invariably a demand for attention and affection.

HOW TO REDUCE BARKING

Useful though barking can be as means of communication, there are also times when most owners wish their pets were less vocal in expressing their feelings and reactions.

A frequently barking dog – especially one who always seems to be barking for no good reason – can be a real nuisance. While it is not a good idea ever to seek to suppress barking in a dog totally – who knows, one day a barked warning could even save your life – there is a lot to be said for trying to moderate it.

Following is a simple but extremely effective way to train your dog so he will bark less frequently.

Because dogs bark for a multitude of reasons and the world abounds with triggers that can set them off, your first trick will be to identify exactly what events cause your dog to bark. Often, this will be reasonably obvious, like the doorbell ringing, the postman shoving mail through the letterbox, or it may just be the sound of children playing nearby.

The next step is to make what professional dog trainers call a 'shake can', a device that consists of nothing more than an ordinary aluminium or steel soft drink can into which you've placed a few small pebbles or some coins before you sealed it shut with a bit of tape across its opening.

Keep your device handy, and the next time your dog begins to regale you with an unwanted – and unwarranted – concert, throw or roll the can in his general direction, making sure you don't actually hit him. Whether you throw or roll, make sure that the can makes a good deal of noise. Almost certainly, the noise will startle the dog and then, now somewhat confused, he will stop barking. As the barking stops, step up to the dog and pat him on the head, telling him what a good dog he is.

Generally, a dozen or so repetitions of this scenario will eventually cause your dog to make two connections in his mind: first of all, inappropriate barking brings a nasty unpleasant noise his way; and, secondly, not barking attracts praise, even, if you're so inclined, a small edible treat.

Almost certainly, this method will ensure that your dog only barks for good reason (when, of course, it should always be allowed to do so).

A 'TAIL' NOTE

When seeking to understand how your dog 'talks', it can be useful to be aware that, apart from being one of his more visible communication tools, your dog's tail also provides him with a number of other most useful biological services. First and foremost perhaps, when the tail is in the down position and part of it is tucked between his legs it acts as a shield that covers the animal's extremely vulnerable hindquarters as well as its sexual parts, and that is the most likely reason why evolution in its wisdom has continued to supply dogs with tails. The tail is also very helpful in various activities, such as serving as an extremely efficient rudder when the dog is swimming; and providing a natural balance-aiding counterweight when he is running or jumping.

Most relevant to us, of course, for the domestic dog, the tail is an invaluable means of communication not just with other dogs but also with his human family.

Usually, the 'basic' tail messages – many of which have been touched upon previously – aren't all that hard to decipher. For example, just about everyone will readily recognise the happy to and fro movement that a contented dog's tail sends out for all to see. And the 'thump, thump' that accompanies an agitated mood is every bit as obvious.

By the way, it's worth noting that the popular expression 'running away with his tail between his legs' is not just graphic but accurately describes exactly what a dog will do when running away because he's frightened. Naturally, the reason why his tail is between his legs is to protect the vulnerable parts already mentioned.

Chapter 6
How To Talk To Your Dog So He Will Understand You

Having learnt, as explained in the previous chapters, how to make good and logical sense of the varied messages that your dog is always sending you is, of course, immensely satisfying. However, achieving that goal, important as it is, is but half the battle.

While it's great to understand dog talk, it's even greater if your dog can also understand *you*. After all, Doctor Dolittle's wish was to 'talk *with* the animals' and not just listen *to* them, and there's absolutely no good reason why you should not be equally ambitious in your aims. After all, any form of communication is ideally a two-way affair!

Just as you had to take into account how dogs express themselves when you were learning their language, you will now have to consider how they learn and how they perceive things if you want them to understand you.

To begin with, and perhaps state the obvious, there is little point in saying, in effect, 'Hey, I went to the trouble to learn dog talk; now it's their turn to learn human talk', as that approach is simply not going to work. No, the bullet that has to be bitten is that if you want to be successful in talking to Rover, you're going to have to do it on his terms. Bright spark though he may be, there are many innate aspects of his makeup that will always severely restrict what you can expect him to learn to understand.

For a clearer appreciation of the limitations that restrict many aspects of man-to-dog talk, you have to explore how a dog's mind works and how his physical senses affect what he can and can't perceive, as we shall now proceed to do.

TWO KEY QUESTIONS ABOUT DIFFERENCES

To achieve empathy with a dog – that is to develop the power to understand and imaginatively enter into his way of thinking and seeing things – two major aspects have to be considered at the outset:

1. What are the major differences between dogs and humans in how they perceive just about every kind of possible stimulus?
2. What are the major differences between dogs and humans in how their minds process the information that has been gleaned about any stimulus?

Of the two questions, the first one is probably the easier to answer because a great deal of painstaking research has been done to establish how a dog's sensory organs differ from ours. The results of these almost innumerable studies are now summarised to give you an idea of the extent to which you have to adapt your thinking if you want to, metaphorically speaking, of course, put yourself in your dog's shoes.

WHAT IS A DOG'S SIGHT LIKE?

It may come as a bit of a surprise to many, but the average dog's eyesight is relatively poor and in fact scores a good deal lower in many respects than that of people with normal vision.

Where dogs do extremely well is in the width of their field of view, also known as peripheral sight. The width of their view will depend upon the breed; the more their eyes are set at the side of their heads, the wider will be the angle. Some dogs will have as much as 270 degrees of view or about three quarters of a full circle which means that while they do not have eyes behind their heads they do have the next best thing. The average field of view for most breeds is more like 200 degrees, still substantially wider than that of people who tend to have around 160 to 170 degrees.

On the other hand, the extent to which dogs can focus their eyes is limited, as compared to that of humans, and most are quite shortsighted. On the plus side, they can see much better than we can in low light conditions as they have a special surface at the back of the eye, behind the retina, that bounces the incoming light back on to the retina thereby almost doubling its luminosity. It is this special surface that can make a dog's eyes look as though they're glowing in the dark.

There is some difference of opinion as to what extent dogs can differentiate between colours. Some experts maintain that dogs are more or less colour-blind, seeing everything in varying shades of grey – somewhat like a Fifties *film noir* – but others say that they can distinguish quite adequately between primary colours, providing these are bright enough. Humans with average vision can of course recognise the full range of colours across what to them is the visible spectrum. One thing is certain and that is whatever may be the exact truth, there is no doubt that colour only plays a small part in a dog's total perception of his universe.

These major differences in vision between dogs and humans are a natural product of evolution, each species gradually developing the kind of sight that was most important to their lifestyles. Man, being of a diurnal disposition, needed sight that worked best in relatively bright light while dogs, who originally were mainly nocturnal animals like their wolf ancestors, required excellent night vision. Over countless generations, Nature adapted the sight of the two species in accordance with these requirements, and dogs ended up with eyes with considerably more rods, the specialised light sensitive cells that enable night vision, while man got a much bigger helping of cones, the cells that amongst other things record fine detail, and eventually emerged with sight that was something like six times better than a dog's for detail.

Two other noteworthy differences in the sight of the two species are:

1. The dog's sight is considerably better than man's at detecting movement.
2. Because of the different positioning of the eyes in the skull, dogs have a considerably narrower *overlap* of vision (that is the area that is seen by both eyes) than humans, the former's overlap being about 100 degrees and the latter's about 140 degrees.

Being aware of how your dog's vision works enables you to take this into account when training or teaching him. For example, it's obvious that there would little point in trying to get him to distinguish between fetching the green or the blue ball when he can hardly see any difference in the hues. Conversely, hand or body movements – which often are an integral part of communicating with your dog – do not have to be pronounced because he will be able to detect even the subtlest of gestures with ease.

YOUR DOG'S HEARING – A TRUE 'SUPER' SENSE

While your dog may not be able to see as well as you can in many respects, his hearing, if normal, will be incomparably better.

An extremely practical example of this will be found in the so-called 'silent' dog whistles that work on the principle of using frequencies so high that we cannot hear them but our pets can. To put this into perspective, a person with good hearing will only recognise sounds up to about 20,000 cycles per second while a dog can pick up sounds with a frequency of up to 35,000 cycles and perhaps even higher. This means that a dog's hearing range can include a full octave higher than ours. Cats, incidentally, do still better with their range extending to an astounding 100,000 cycles per second. To give you an idea of how high this is you can compare it to the highest C note on a standard 88-note piano, which will vibrate, if tuned correctly, 4,224 times per second. But even more astonishing than the pitch range of their hearing is how acutely dogs can detect the most minute of sounds, it having been reliably estimated that a level of sound a human can just barely discern at 100 yards away would still be clearly audible to a dog at a distance of a quarter mile.

Several important points emerge from the above:

❑ Your dog's extremely keen sense of hearing means that in even a comparatively quiet household he is living in what can seem to him like a fairly noisy environment. This explains why your pet may often react strongly to noises that we would think of as only moderately loud, because to him these sounds represent a veritable assault on the most sensitive of his senses.

❑ Your dog's extremely acute hearing also explains why he may do something seemingly inexplicable at times, such as suddenly getting up and roaming inquisitively around the house. This kind of behaviour is usually the result of his sensitive ears having picked up a sound that's well beyond our hearing and he's trying to locate its source.

❑ As far as training your dog is concerned, including trying to get him to understand your verbal commands, you should take into account the sensitivity of his hearing by only speaking to him quite softly, as even raising your voice only slightly above the level of normal conversation will sound incredibly loud, perhaps even painful, to him, thereby distracting rather than focusing his attention on what you're saying.

What have been described above are the attributes of a dog with broadly normal hearing. Sadly, however, deafness is a condition that afflicts many dogs, but the following notes will help you to train a pet whose hearing is impaired.

To begin with the good news, deafness is quite uncommon in younger dogs, with the exception of certain breeds such as the white Bull Terrier in which the condition is congenital, and that very few puppies are born deaf. The bad news is that senile deafness does affect many dogs as they become older with the first symptoms usually manifesting themselves from the age of about nine years onwards.

As with humans, the older dog usually first loses the ability to hear the higher frequencies . . . something that, incidentally, means the end of the usefulness of the so-called silent whistle. Gradually the hearing will continue to deteriorate until the dog hears very little, if anything at all. Much can be done by a caring owner for a dog who is losing his hearing and most pets adapt very well to their handicap. However, extra care must be taken with road traffic, as the dog will no longer hear the noise of an oncoming car.

By the way, deafness may also be temporary, caused by an accumulation of wax in the ear. The home treatment for this is to pour a small amount of warm, not hot, olive oil into the ear so that it eventually, perhaps over the course of several treatments, softens the wax sufficiently to allow it to come out naturally. Don't try anything more drastic if your pet fails to respond to this treatment and on no account ever poke about in his ears.

Suspected deafness should always be referred to a vet as it

may be caused by infection of the ear canal, middle ear or inner ear, all of which need professional diagnosis and help.

As far as training a dog that is either deaf or gradually becoming so is concerned, you have to reconsider many aspects to the language you're using to communicate with him, as verbal commands are going to be of little use. The answer is to rely instead on commands that are conveyed by signs, such as a downward wave of your hand with the palm down signalling 'Sit' or you gently slapping the side of your thigh meaning 'It's time for walkies, let's put your collar on.' Additionally, whether you are consciously aware of this or not, you probably already use certain tell-tale body stances when you're telling a hearing dog something, and, should he become deaf in later years, he will probably be able to relate your various body positions to the words that he would have heard had he been able to do so.

A SUPERLATIVE SENSE OF SMELL

While the eyesight of dogs is not that much to write home about and their hearing is excellent, their sense of smell really puts them at the very top of any class. Sadly, this extremely highly developed sense is usually of little practical purpose when it comes to training dogs as you can hardly be expected to produce message-laden scents on demand.

Just the same, to give you a more rounded picture of how your pet interacts with his world, here are a few details about how well equipped he is to detect the very faintest of odours.

For starters, experts say that a dog's sense of smell is so powerful that it can be correctly stated that it is his most important sense as compared to humans who rely primarily on sight and for whom smells are usually comparatively unimportant.

This means that your pet lives constantly in an environment that abounds with all kinds of aromas, most of which we would be unable to detect even if we were to put our noses directly on top of their sources. This uncanny ability to fetch and recognise even a few molecules of a smell out of the air naturally explains why tracking dogs are so successful and can follow a trail just by picking up their quarry's trail.

Partly because his eyesight isn't the greatest, your dog depends greatly on smells as sources of information about what surrounds him, and you only have to observe your pet running off the lead in a park to see how important smells are to him. Nose close to the ground, he'll sniff this and that, and then bound off again to follow an elusive or particularly attractive scent. For him, the smells are truly the scenery!

JUST HOW INTELLIGENT IS YOUR DOG?

While the relative sensitivities of a dog's various senses govern what information he gets from what surrounds him, this information still has to be processed by his brain before it can be of any use to him. Obvious though that statement may be, it automatically begs another all-important question: exactly how intelligent are our canine friends?

There's no easy answer to this seemingly simple query, because it is a subject about which the experts hold a wide diversity of views.

At one extreme, there are those who argue that dogs have no intelligence as such and merely have varied degrees of capabilities in handling different tasks, these mainly the result of instinct, breeding or training. These people also point out that dogs can't grasp even the simplest of principles and have nothing that even faintly resembles human reasoning powers.

Other experts, equally learned, hold a diametrically opposed view and say that dogs are highly intelligent. These people usually support their opinion by citing the established fact that most dogs are extremely quick students who can and do learn from experience.

The truth of the matter is perhaps somewhat more elusive as it depends to a large extent on what you really mean by 'intelligence'. The dictionary defines it as 'the capacity for understanding; an ability to perceive and comprehend meaning', in which case, of course, dogs may well fall pretty low on the I.Q. scale. But another common interpretation – and perhaps a better one in this context – of intelligence is to use the word to describe a capacity for acquiring information and then making rational use of it. And that surely is exactly what a dog does when he absorbs the training he's given and then proceeds to act accordingly.

Many owners do tend to confuse intelligence with obedience, but the two are not necessarily connected and just because your pet is of a particularly submissive nature and slavishly tries to obey your every command that doesn't mean that he's got a high I.Q. In fact, there's a strong argument to be made for the contrary view by saying that a really bright dog, perhaps somewhat like a precocious human youngster, is likely to be of a more independent turn of mind than his less intelligent counterpart and so will not necessarily be so malleable.

Although there are numerous tests designed to gauge a dog's intelligence, they really aren't all that reliable or useful in practical terms, often being more of a divertissement than a genuinely scientific appraisal. However, if you're determined to find out just how bright your dog is, there is a fairly simple way to at least get a broad idea of how brightly his bulb is burning. This is what you do (assuming that, as every good dog owner should, you've already taught Fido to unhesitatingly obey the command 'sit'):

❏ When you have your dog's attention, gently clap your hands together two times, and then issue the command to sit. If, as expected, your pet obeys, praise him and give him a small treat.

❑ Perform this routine ten times running in fairly quick succession.

❑ On the eleventh occasion, only clap your hands twice without adding the command to sit.

❑ If Fido does indeed sit, having learned the connection between hand clapping and sitting down without also needing the accompanying command after only ten repetitions of the teaching routine, you're blessed with a really bright dog, one that absorbs new knowledge very quickly.

❑ Should your dog fail to sit in response to just the hand claps, then go through the routine ten more times and try again, and, if necessary, continue with further repetitions of sets of ten until the message does get through to him.

To assess how well your pet fares in the canine I.Q. stakes, rate him as follows: if he sits in response to only the hand claps after only one set of instruction, he's a furry Einstein; if it takes him about five sets to grasp what he should do, he's more or less average; more than twenty sets means that you'd best not enter him for Mastermind.

Light-hearted though this test is, it nevertheless can be a reasonably good indicator of your dog's relative intelligence. Even so don't despair if your dog fails to come top of the class, because he may well have other outstanding attributes that more than make up for his failure to do all that well in this particular testing procedure that is admittedly very limited in its scope.

PUTTING THEORY INTO PRACTICE

Now that you have obtained a pretty good insight into your dog's 'world', the next step is to put that knowledge to practical use, as will be explained in the next chapter.

Chapter 7
Training Your Dog So He Will Understand You Better

When you set out to train your dog so that he can eventually have a greater and better understanding of what you're telling him, you must always remember that the process involved is a dual one. Success will depend just as much upon how you approach it as it does on your dog's ability to learn to understand what you're trying to tell him.

In the previous chapter, we have explored the many physical and mental differences that cause dogs to be unable to perceive correctly or process many forms of human communication. Keeping these restrictions in mind, we will now look at a number of different ways through which you can ensure that both talking *to* and *with* your dog will always be as effective as possible.

CONSISTENCY AT ALL TIMES

The very first thing you must train yourself to do when setting out to establish better communications with your dog is to be *utterly consistent* at all times. Consistency is probably the single greatest aid to learning and it's quite understandable why that should be so. After all, a lack of consistency when you're talking to your dog means that you're sending him messages that, by definition, can at times be self-contradictory, but you are expecting him to make sense of them. Think for a moment about how confused you would be if words – sounds to your dog – were to mean something specific at one moment but take on a totally different meaning on another occasion.

Write it on the door of your fridge, enter it on every page of your diary, do whatever it takes to remember it, but always follow this Golden Rule: *To avoid creating confusion in your dog's mind, you always have to be totally consistent in your dealings with him.*

Naturally, if there are other people in your household, they should also be equally consistent when they're taking to/with your pet or dealing with him in other ways. And, of course, there should be agreement between the human members of the household as to what words they use when talking to your dog, as anything else can only create confusion in his mind. For example, it's a good idea to decide amongst yourselves whether everyone will use the command 'sit' or 'sit down', or whether feeding time will be announced as 'dinner' or 'din-dins'. Asking your dog to relate two or more different sounds to the same concept can only lead to a loss of clarity.

THE RIGHT TONE OF VOICE AND CHOICE OF WORDS

Dogs will respond best when talked to in a moderately soft and somewhat monotonous tone of voice. No matter how greatly you may be tempted, because of some irritating behaviour on his part, don't ever shout at your pet. This will only make him agitated and completely destroy his concentration. Repetition can help if you use the same words over and over again under similar circumstances, as your pet will learn to associate the sound of a particular phrase with a certain kind of event.

Other points to note in this context:

❑ Because a dog's hearing is so much more sensitive than ours, even raising your voice ever so slightly above a normal conversational level may make him think that you're shouting at him.

❑ With some dogs – not all, by any means – you may get a better level of sound recognition if you pronounce words, even if they only have one syllable, with a slight variation in pitch. Elongating the vowel sounds, as singers often do, may also help.

❑ When you're deciding on a new command or instruction, look for a suitable word that has meaning for you but which, insofar as this is possible, does sound quite differently from other words you've already taught your pet to recognise. For example, if the new command is meant to ask him to extend his forepaw to, as it were, shake hands, choose 'shake' instead of 'paw' if he has already learned to associate 'Grandpa' with a member of your household.

AVOID THE TRAP OF ANTHROPOMORPHISM

Attempts at communication with a pet can often fail because the owner has expected an almost human response from his four-legged friend. 'Anthropomorphism' is the big word used to describe what happens when people start to attribute human qualities and attributes to their dogs. While that is something we all do now and then – 'Fido is so clever, I would swear he's almost human' – it can lead to serious misunderstandings and greatly hamper the establishment of better communication in some circumstances.

Because dogs are not little humans in fur coats, they don't think, react and have emotions in the same way as we do . . . which is not to say that they don't think, react or have emotions. They certainly do, but in a very different manner.

You're guilty of anthropomorphism when you try to explain

to your pet that he should stop running around the house and settle down 'because it's late and we're all very tired'. On a more serious level, the same thing happens when you try to use human logic to understand your dog's behaviour, a sure way to get off on the wrong track.

To avoid anthropomorphic behaviour on your part, always remember that it is you who should try to think like a dog if you want to achieve successful two-way communication, and not expect the dog to start thinking as you do.

SOUNDS HAVE MEANINGS, WORDS DON'T

This statement may come as a little bit of a shock to many devoted dog lovers, but there's no evidence whatsoever to support the idea that any dog has *ever* understood a single word as such. Dogs are, however, incredibly good at understanding the *meaning* of what you say – and the distinction between a word and its meaning is vital to your understanding of how your dog interprets and reacts to what you tell him.

Say, for example, that every time you are preparing his food you call him by saying 'Dinner, dinner' in a certain tone of voice and with a certain inflection. Your pet will soon learn to associate the sound you make with his food being served up. Now, if some time later you were to say instead 'Winter, winter' using the same tone and inflection, the chances are high that your dog will react exactly as though you had said 'Dinner, dinner'.

It follows from the above that it's therefore quite useless to string two or more words together to make a sentence and expect your pet to understand the *combined* meaning of the words. However, what you may be able to do is to speak one word – for example 'sit' – and then follow this quite quickly with another such as 'basket' – and your dog just might realise that the command to 'sit' is, as it were, *modified* by the word that followed it and, accordingly, happily plonk himself in his basket instead of on the floor.

Just because dogs cannot understand words does not mean that there is not a great deal to be gained from talking to – as well as *with* – your dog. In fact, whenever you're doing something for your pet, feeding him, grooming him, playing with him, it's a very good idea to talk to him at the same time. While, at first, this conversation may seem very much one-sided, you'll soon realise that it isn't and that while your dog isn't answering in words he is none the less responding in less obvious but nevertheless clear ways to what you're saying.

Watch your pet's eyes as you stroke his head and talk to him and you'll see a perfect example of this sort of behaviour as he looks at you as though he is trying to decipher what you're saying. And that is exactly what he is doing, trying to understand not the words – that's not really within his intellectual grasp – but the meaning of your message. Given half a chance, he'll succeed in interpreting your mood extremely accurately most of the time and will respond accordingly.

As with most things, practice makes perfect, and the more you talk to your dog, the more responsive and understanding he will become. Of equal importance is the fact that your dog will almost certainly also become more communicative and 'talk' back to you in his fashion. As we already know, dogs mainly express themselves through body movements and changes in expression, all of these sending messages that you can interpret.

HOW YOUR PET'S EXCELLENT MEMORY HELPS HIM UNDERSTAND YOU

When you try to communicate with your pet, always keep in mind what his capabilities to understand you really are. And to bring this point home, it's worth quoting Dr Alan Walker, the

Consultant Scientific Adviser to Spillers Foods, who wrote: 'We must accept that a dog's mental ability, though far greater than was realised until recently, is severely limited. A dog's senses, except for sight, are superior to ours. He has an excellent memory for events and is very observant but a dog cannot understand abstract concepts. He does not think about past events or try to predict the future. He does not understand the reasons for being ill or that he will die one day. Above all, he has not the faintest idea why he carries out the numerous tasks we train him to do. He carries them out because he has been trained and is pleased to do this because of the pleasure we display and the caresses or other rewards he receives. A trained dog is our loyal, obedient but unreasoning servant'.

It is worth elaborating on Dr Walker's remarks, in particular the ones about the dog's excellent memory and powers of observation. Your pet's remarkable memory is one of the keys that can unlock better communication between you, as your dog will always try to relate what you're saying or doing today to similar matching events in the past. Therefore, as already mentioned, one of the golden rules is that of consistency, because dogs do not only learn by repetition but are also creatures of habit, so will respond best in an environment where the same things happen more or less at the same time of the day and are accompanied by similar 'noises', which is how he hears the words you may speak to him.

Another important point made by Dr Walker concerns how very observant your dog can be. Doubtlessly, like every other dog owner, you will have seen your pet sitting quietly in a corner while he follows your every move as you busy yourself with everyday tasks. At that moment your dog is storing events in his memory and if you were to speak to him during those times, repeating the pattern time and time again, he would start to link the sounds you make with whatever is happening at the time. Gradually, quite a varied vocabulary can be established this way – not a vocabulary of actual words, of course – but one of sounds that your dog automatically links to certain happenings. And when a sound means an event and the event brings the expected sound, you're to all intents and purposes actually talking not just to but also with your dog!

There is yet another very good reason why you should spend time talking with your pet and that is that dogs can very quickly become lonely. Being a pack animal, your dog longs for companionship and the sound of your voice will be reassuring to him as he sees you as the leader of the pack.

BARKING IS STRICTLY FOR DOGS AND NOT FOR HUMANS

Another important aspect of this subject concerns the sounds your dog may produce as he talks back to you. Although many people are quite good at imitating the barks of dogs and even thereby elicit responses of sorts, nobody can claim to truly understand what the various sounds mean – apart from the extremely obvious ones. Naturally, if you don't know exactly what a particular barking sound means, then there is little point in trying to copy it. Even if you managed to get it so accurate that your dog might recognise it, you wouldn't really know what you were saying.

Additionally, there is another good reason why most experts agree that barking at your dog in the hope that he will understand you is not a very clever thing to do. Bark at your pet, and it's likely that instead of establishing communications you will just be upsetting your pet who may even as a result become one of those rather annoying dogs who are always barking for no particular reason. Accordingly, when you're talking with your dog, leave simulated barking out of your repertoire, as trying to speak 'dog language' that way will almost certainly be counterproductive.

RULES ARE FOR HUMANS ONLY

Many dog owners somehow seem to think that dogs can learn to understand rules, then they are surprised when their poor Rover does something they thought he knew was very much 'against the rules'. Of course, what happened is that poor Rover, who had been trained not to sit on the living-room sofa, didn't realise that this injunction was part of a general rule that also forbade him from sitting on the bed.

To understand a rule – which means 'a principle to which action must conform' – is a concept that's quite beyond your dog's ability to reason. In fact, it's a concept that even humans generally can't begin to grasp until they're three or four or even five years old. So forget the notion of laying down rules of behaviour for your pet; but rather have them for your own sake – to ensure that all-important consistency in *your* behaviour towards him – without expecting him to understand them.

To your dog every action is a thing in itself, that through training, including correction or reward, he will have learned to classify as leading to something nice or something unpleasant. However, it is unreasonable to expect him to project this learning process to encompass other actions that you think of as broadly similar.

THE KEYS TO A DOG'S LEARNING PROCESS

The golden principle always to bear in mind when trying to teach a dog anything – including getting him to understand the meaning behind the words you use to speak to him – is to remember that the keys to his learning process are twofold, consisting, first of all, of association of ideas and, secondly, of correction or reward.

And it is by the correct application of correction or reward following certain types of behaviour that your pet will start making the kind of associations of ideas that will reinforce the correct or desired behaviour. This means that if Fido does a 'good' thing, reward him there and then; if he's 'naughty', also immediately let him know of your displeasure. If this happens enough times, without deviations, your dog will soon learn what behaviour leads to a reward and quite naturally and selfishly will begin to behave accordingly.

A very important point is that any reward or correction must be applied *immediately* when the behaviour takes place. It's no good scolding your pet if you come home and find he's tipped over a vase of flowers during your absence. In his mind, he won't associate your displeasure with the vase he toppled some hours previously but will instead link it to your coming home. And that's how you might end up with a pet that cowers away the moment he hears you opening the front door!

'Correction', of course, doesn't mean beating the poor animal but instead putting across a reprimand that typically might consist of taking a firm hold of him, looking straight into his face and scolding him. If he happens to be on a lead at the time when he needs to be corrected, then it's usually enough to give the lead a sharp jerk as he attempts the undesirable behaviour.

The reward part can be provided in two main ways. Small titbits of food are used for this to good effect by most owners; although many experts frown on that practice saying that a friendly pat on the head and making a fuss of your pet is every bit as effective.

Most owners find that the best system is a combination of using both titbits and praise, matching the chosen reward to the situation and their particular dog. But whatever kind of reward you decide to use, its timing is vitally important and it must be given just as the desired action takes place or immediately after it has been completed. If you're a bit slow in delivering the reward the chances are that your dog won't associate it with the previous behaviour and just see it as a welcome bonus you've added to his usual fare.

One other thing to keep in mind is that the reward, while pleasant, should not over-excite your dog and so take his mind off the training. A dog who really loves bits of cheese may become over-excited if they're given to him and in that case it's perhaps better to reward him more modestly with lots of praise and a congratulatory pat on the head.

ALL DOGS ARE NOT EQUAL

The ability of dogs to learn new things is by no means equal. However, they can to a greater or lesser extent invariably learn to understand what you're telling them, providing you put in the necessary effort to make this as clear as possible. Equally, just about all dogs – unless they're affected by a pathological condition – can learn the basics of being a household pet, such as being clean, going for walks, and not biting the hand that feeds them. However, training for some specific purposes – such as becoming a gun dog, a guard dog, a police dog, or herding sheep – is not suitable for all dogs. If you want a dog that can be expected to do these specialist tasks well, you must choose one from a breed whose proven capabilities match your particular requirements.

One particular skill that can be acquired by almost all breeds is retrieving although, as expected, the specialist breeds will perform better than the average pet.

For everyday purposes the training that can be given to a dog depends mainly upon his personality and character. The more dominant the animal is, the more difficult your task will be as your main ally in teaching him anything is the dog's strong submissive instinct which will make him want to please you, who he sees as his pack leader.

This means that, of course, the other major factor to achieving success is you, his trainer, and your approach to his training programme. That perhaps more than anything else will determine how much fruit your efforts will bear in the long run. One last point worth mentioning is that like 'horses for courses', dogs are also very individualistic and you may well find that your dog learns so-called hard things easily and easy things slowly.

HOW SOON SHOULD I BEGIN TEACHING MY PUPPY TO UNDERSTAND ME?

The sooner the better is the short answer to that question, and this also applies to all other aspects of training. It used to be commonly believed that there was little point in starting training of any kind until a puppy was at least four or so months old. Now, as a result of carefully controlled scientific research, the consensus of opinion has shifted considerably, and it now seems that six weeks is the optimum age at which to begin training your puppy.

Of course, what a puppy can be taught at such an early age is limited. But, according to the experts, it's not so much what he learns but the kind of learning environment the owner provides that matters. Perhaps the most important lesson of all that a puppy must learn at an early age is that his owner's wishes will always prevail over his. In other words, don't give in to him, but keep making it clear that you're his pack leader.

The first crucial battle, say the experts, is most likely to take place on the very first night when you've just brought a puppy into your home. Separated from his mother and the rest of his litter, the pup will be upset and disorientated and, as you go to bed leaving him alone, he will kick up a fuss. No matter how much the pup may whine, yap and howl, ignore it! For, should you give in to his complaints and go to comfort him, he will have learned that creating a row brings him what he wants – one of the very worst lessons that any dog can ever learn. If, however, you don't respond to his fussing he will eventually get tired of it and eventually drift off to sleep. Two or three nights of this scenario will be enough for the pup to learn that creating a ruckus achieves exactly nothing and that therefore he may as well not bother and save his breath. By being steadfast in your refusal to be controlled by his actions, you will have won the first battle of wills and started his training off on the right foot.

Naturally, as you gradually train your puppy in various matters always make 'conversation', limited though it may at the outset, part of the curriculum. The more frequently your dog hears your voice as you interact together, the sooner he will start making sense of the sounds he hears.

IS A DOG EVER TOO OLD TO LEARN NEW TRICKS?

While any kind of training of a dog ideally starts when he is still a youngster, this isn't always possible, as many people adopt older dogs that may well already have acquired a set of bad habits. This raises a question about whether it is truly possible to change behaviour patterns in an older dog that is pretty set in his ways.

Despite what the proverb says about old dogs and new tricks, the fact is that you can successfully instil new behaviours in a mature dog, as well as eradicate some old, undesirable ones, but it will take a great deal of understanding, perseverance and patience. And the proverb is correct enough when it implies that the older the dog the more arduous your task will be. Although any training is most successful when a dog is young and his mind is receptive, a mature dog can learn all kinds of new things – and this most certainly also includes developing an understanding of what the sound of various human words mean as far as he is concerned.

Many times, a big part of the problem will be that your dog will not just have to learn something new but will also have to 'un-learn' something else. Take the example of Bingo, a six-year-old Cocker Spaniel, who since puppyhood had spent his nights comfortably curled up at the bottom of his master's bed. When his owner developed a bad back, it no longer seemed such a good idea to share sleeping arrangements and Bingo had to learn that his new bed was a basket beside the bed.

The way that 'old' Bingo learned his 'new' trick was initially by placing the basket on the bed so he got used to it and then moving it on to a coffee table beside the bed and eventually on to the floor. What happened was that an old pattern – Bingo sleeping on the bed – was first of all modified – sleeping in the basket on the bed – and then modified again – Bingo in the basket that was first beside the bed before it finally rested on the floor. This example illustrates the kind of thinking you'll have to use to alter successfully well-established behaviour. Do it bit by bit, altering one element at a time until you finally achieve the desired result.

Exactly the same principle – that of introducing change gradually, one little bit at a time – can be applied most successfully to introducing a slightly superannuated Fido to the mystery of making sense of all the strange sounds his human pack leader keeps making.

Chapter 8
In Conclusion

As we near the end of this book, there are some less immediately practical and perhaps more philosophical questions that still need to be addressed. These concern the whole concept of what underlies the man and dog relationship and also influence to a large extent the ability of the two species to achieve meaningful communication.

Like in any partnership, in an ideal world both of those involved in it would get equal, or at least more or less equal, benefits from their mutual arrangement. Naturally, this is not always the case, and in most instances it can be safely said that either the dog or his master come out ahead from the deal. That's perhaps fair enough, but when you're trying to establish the best of all possible relationships, as well as optimum two-way communications, with your pet, it can be valuable to be aware of exactly what the relationship entails and who gets what out of it.

To begin with, let's look at what dogs – and here we are talking essentially about dogs that are kept as family pets, not working dogs – get, or hope to get, from humans.

People of a slightly cynical bent would quickly answer that question by saying that dogs get free food, free shelter, warmth and affection from their owners and wonder what more could these pampered animals possibly want.

Much of that view is true enough as far as it goes. But there is a good deal more to owning a dog than just providing for his physical comfort. There is no doubt that, on a much deeper level, dogs also have a strong psychological need for their owners to be their leaders, and meeting that need is also a very important part of the human owner's responsibility. As descendants from pack animals, dogs truly need to be guided by a leader and it is our good fortune that they're usually quite willing to accept a human owner in this role. This is one of the reasons why early training that unequivocally establishes you as the boss is truly vital for the proper development of any dog and owner relationship.

Just as dogs need people, many people also need dogs, and when the right combination of the two gets together it can result in a bond that's unlike any other. Few people would doubt that of all the animals, the dog is the one best equipped to provide companionship for his human owner (though you just might get a spirited argument about this from a dedicated cat lover!). Treat your canine friend kindly and lovingly – as well as correctly – and he will reward you with that very special kind of devotion and love that only a dog can offer. What more can you reasonably expect to get from any relationship?

And, on a lighter note, to assist you into becoming the ideal kind of owner your dog would like you to be, you may wish to take account of the following suggestions . . .

DOGS' GOLDEN RULES FOR OWNERS

Were dogs able to express their wishes in writing, these are some of the points they would like incorporated in A Dog's Charter of Rules for Owners, according to suggestions posted on various web sites by dog lovers.

❑ I will not drag my dog off to an enforced bath every time after he has been playing in a mud puddle. Neither will I refuse him a heartfelt hug just because he's covered with mud.

☐ I will not stand gawking at him as he attends to his outdoor toilet needs but will discreetly look away. And I shan't try to drag him away from his favourite tree or lamppost until he had had plenty of time to fully attend to business, including such sniffing that he deems necessary.

☐ Unless the weather is really foul, I shall not leave the house without taking him with me. (This rule may be disregarded now and then for certain outside human activities – such as going to work or to the dentist – which probably would hold little interest anyway for a sensible dog.)

☐ If I leave my dog on his own when I go to work, I won't wake him when I come home but will tiptoe around the house until he's good and ready to emerge from his well-deserved sleep.

☐ Whenever my dog wants to go for a walk, I shall without hesitation set aside whatever I may be doing to attend to his wish.

☐ When out for walkies, I will let my dog set the pace and itinerary, stopping and doubling back as many times as he wants me to.

☐ I will always feed my dog before I feed myself, and I'll give him the opportunity to share with me everything I eat before I taste a morsel.

☐ I will always be ready to open the back door just as soon as my dog goes and sits near it.

☐ My pockets will always contain an assortment of doggie treats and I will never allow these to run out.

☐ When playing ball or any other game, I shan't use feeble excuses like 'My arm is so tired that it's about ready to drop off' or 'I have this terrible shooting pain up my back' to stop play before he, too, is dog-tired and wants to call it a day.

❑ Lastly, I will never, but never, substitute a boomerang for the ball or stick when playing fetch with my dog.

BOWLINGUAL – A POINTER TO THE FUTURE?

Finally, to end this book with a glimpse into a possible future, it's worth mentioning that some day there could be an easier way to interpret at least part of your dog's language.

A major Japanese manufacturer of toys – Takara, which is now part of the omnipresent Tomy group – has been working hard to create a device that will eventually, or so it is claimed, allow easy one-way communication between dogs and humans through the intermediary of a portable electronic 'translation machine'.

Although the project is still in its early stages, a Mark One version of the device – called Bowlingual – has been produced and is said to be selling well in Japan.

In use, the Bowlingual device, which looks rather like a small plastic egg with a miniature LCD display screen and a few buttons, is connected to a microphone that is then attached to the dog's collar. Whenever the dog barks, the microphone picks up the sound and sends it to the device that then interprets the meaning of the bark through its 'Animal Emotion Analysis System' and displays the result of its findings, together with a relevant cartoon depiction of a dog, on the screen.

In its current stage of development, Bowlingual only relates barks to half a dozen emotional states, these including happiness, sadness, pleasure, aggression and so on. Additionally, the strength of the currently expressed emotion is also graded according to a scale that is displayed as well.

Each of the six basic emotional states recognised by the device is associated with fixed equivalents expressed in human language. So, for example, a particular bark may be translated as 'Please leave me alone, I want to sleep now' while another will be interpreted as 'I am getting ready to bite you, so watch out'.

The device also has a special mode that records the dog's barks while its owner is away. Called Bow Wow Diary, this mode collects information about the dog's varying emotional states over a period of time and then presents these in graph form on the screen.

'This is only the beginning of what we hope to eventually achieve with Bowlingual', said a spokesman for Takara. 'Future models will cope with much finer nuances of dog talk, and will also incorporate a Bowlingual Mail System that will let the device send email messages to an absent owner telling him how their dog is reacting emotionally while being left on its own.'

Takara, the spokesman added, was also working on a much wider research project – appropriately enough called 'Dolittle' – aimed at improving through electronic sound analysis all aspects of human communication with animals of various species, including dogs, cats, horses and different kinds of birds.

While, judging by what has been achieved so far by Bowlingual, later models may become a genuinely useful aid in understanding what dogs say, it still remains a fact that most of what your dog is telling you is conveyed by other than verbal signals. Until the day comes that an electronic device can also interpret animal body language, human owners will still have to learn dog talk the old-fashioned way – that is, mainly by constant observation, memorisation and interpretation.